YOU CAN MAKE IT
— IN —
MUSIC

David Grossman

Copyright © 2024 David Grossman

All rights reserved.

No part of this book may be reproduced, or stored in a retrieval system,
or transmitted in any form or by any means, electronic, mechanical, photocopying, recording, or otherwise, without express written permission
of the publisher.

ISBN: 979-8-218-36906-4

Library of Congress Control Number: 2024900341
Published in Santa Barbara, California
Printed in the United States of America

For further information, visit:
Youcanmakeitinmusic.com

Contents

What This Book Is All About 1
Music Gigs-A-Plenty 6
Delete Your Plan "B" 14
Big Bite-Sized Ideas 16
May Luck Be With You 34
Positivity 36
Top Secret - For Your Mind Only 39
Powerwords 41
Thick Skin 42
Let's Get Motivated 45
I'll Do It Tomorrow 47
Standing On The Shoulders Of Others 49
The Music Business Is The People Business 51
You Are Not Alone 55
The Business Of Music 57
Why The Heck Not 67
To Music College – Or Not 69
The World Of Musical Styles 77
The Superstars Speak 80
Math/Schmath! 84
Be A Body Builder 87
Stories From the Real World 91
Bonus Topics (mainly) For Instrumentalists and Vocalists 98
The Overtone Series 106
The Whole Story 109
To Sum It All Up 137
With Great Appreciation and Admiration 138

Dedication

To Sam Bruce, who taught me how to read music in 5th grade and had a sign over his chalkboard that read: "Success is the result of effort." He was right.

To Herb Allen, a powerhouse of a musician and human being whose infectious love of people and music fueled my commitment to a music career. His talent and wisdom enriched generations of young people worldwide and I was incredibly fortunate to have been able to call him a friend.

Thank you both for inspiring this book, and I'll see you again "Where the roads come together."

And especially to my mom and dad for always supporting me, no matter how crazy it seemed. None of this would have happened without their unconditional love and support.

About the Author

Rochester, New York native David Grossman was nine years old when he picked up drumsticks and fell in love with music. He aspired to teach at his junior high school and play an occasional weekend gig as an adult, but his ambitions evolved. By 17 he was on the road performing globally with an international musical production and by 23 he held a degree from the prestigious Berklee College of Music, which would later honor him with their Distinguished Alumni Award. David later earned an MBA from Pepperdine University.

Transitioning to a successful run as a studio musician in Los Angeles, he eventually shifted focus and became head of TV music at Columbia Pictures Television/Sony. There, he honed his skills as a creative and business executive, supervising music for dozens of television series and movies-of-the week.

David's next position in the entertainment industry, which he held for 17 years, was Senior Vice President of Music for Paramount Pictures Television. In that role he executive-produced 13 television soundtrack albums while overseeing the complex challenge of generating thousands of hours of television music heard worldwide, crossing paths with such artistic luminaries as Quincy Jones, Ringo Starr, Roger Daltrey, Phil Ramone, Kenny (Babyface) Edmunds, Diane Warren, Art Garfunkel, Stanley Clarke, David Foster, Keb' Mo', Richie Sambora, Jimmy Jam, and others.

In addition, David spent five years as Executive Vice-President of the Recording Academy, best known for the Grammy Awards, before becoming Executive Director of the Santa Barbara Symphony.

David's career continues to evolve. As a contributing writer to the international publication *Astronomy Magazine,* he blends the subject of music with his longtime passion for stargazing, while continuing his interest in drums, composing and music education.

He currently lives with his wife in Santa Barbara, California.

What This Book Is All About

It could be a book on how to write songs or become a rock star.
It could be a book on how to get a record or publishing deal.
It could be a book on how to DJ or produce records.
It could be a book on how to be a symphonic or studio musician.
It could be a book on how to compose for video games or TV.

Because it *is* a book about how to succeed in all those professions and at <u>anything</u> else in music you can possibly imagine!

Let me explain.

This book is about imagining and creating possibilities using timeless ideas to ignite the future you want. Some call it your outlook, attitude, mindset, or frame of mind, but success begins with how you *think* and the conscious steps you take.

This book is about recognizing abilities and talents that <u>only</u> you uniquely have so you can customize your future to fit whatever resonates with you.

This book is about mental preparation and gaining unlimited confidence and trust in yourself so that you can find success that makes you happy within the music industry.

What This Book Is All About

You're already in love with music and want to explore your career opportunities or you wouldn't be reading this, but the inevitable question will arise:

"What are the odds of my having a long-term and successful career in music?"

Let me ask you this: If you think a music career is what you really want, why not ask:

"What are all the reasons I expect to make it in music!?"

For many, a career in music is about playing an instrument and hoping you can make a living at it. And while many people in the music industry play an instrument to some degree or another, it's definitely not a prerequisite to be successful in music.

Fine-tuning your mental skill set and creating a unique combination of building blocks is at your fingertips with this book. And while technology, business models and music delivery systems, etc., have changed, and will continue to change dramatically over the years, the human nature constants in this book most likely won't.

This book includes what worked for me, but my journey is just that - mine. No one will ever have the identical path again - in the same way that no one will ever have the same life experiences, opportunities or challenges you have had - and will have.

My path allowed a guy from Rochester, New York, who only aspired to teach music at his junior high school and play gigs on the weekend to end up with a successful music career in Hollywood, California. But this is about <u>you</u> and your dreams; those currently imagined and those yet to hit your radar.

I hope these pages are a resource in your "toolbox" as you strive for a limitless and fulfilling music career. My goal is for you to have a few "Aha" or "Eureka" moments - those moments when a sudden insight that wasn't there previously - rushes into your thoughts.

What This Book Is All About

When I was thinking about a music career, I understood all the stuff that came naturally, like practicing, playing with bands, and listening to music. Still, it was what I didn't know that I wish I could have known. Of course, I didn't know what I didn't know, so there was no way for me to know it! But these days there are many ways to get a head start and I'm hopeful this book becomes one of those ways for you.

In a nutshell, this is the book I wish I could have read when I was dreaming about a music career. Think of it as a possible compass for you to use - since life doesn't come with a map.

I am so excited to share it with you now!

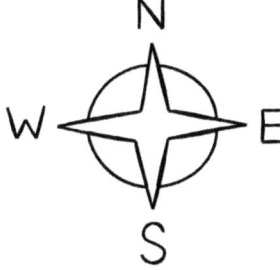

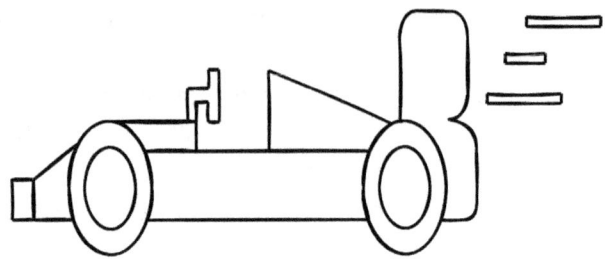

Quick Start

You're here because you want to make music your career. And you can do it!

I did it, although not in the way I ever imagined I would.

I want to share what I learned with you.

Here's a snapshot about me:

I was 9 when I picked up drumsticks and fell in love with music.

By 13, music had become my passion and career goal.

At 17, I was on the road touring internationally as a musician.

By 23, I had a music degree from Berklee College of Music.

At 24, I began a career as a freelance musician in Los Angeles, California.

At 30, I was the Music Supervisor for Columbia Pictures Television in Hollywood, California.

At 33 (and for the next 17 years), I was Senior Vice President for Paramount Pictures Television Music, supervising music heard globally and executive producing 13 soundtrack albums - followed by an appointment as the Executive Vice President of the organization best known for the Grammy Awards.

If you're interested in how all of this actually happened, please read the chapter, aptly called "The Whole Story."

Of course, you are welcome to randomly jump to any part of the book since each chapter has unique ideas that don't need to be read in any particular order. And some chapters will be more applicable to you than others.

Lastly, it's more of a personal career guide than a book. Write on it, doodle on it, and cross out things that don't apply to you or circle things you'd like to return to.

And one last thing...

Sometimes other people's words can inspire you or your creativity, so throughout this book I have sprinkled my favorite quotes that have done just that.

They're inside a border that looks like this:

Ok, now...

Let's do this!

Music Gigs-A-Plenty

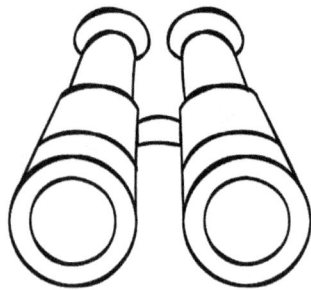

Given the title of this book, I'm going to jump right into the topic of music careers. But once you've got the idea that there are *a lot* of ways to make it in the world of music, keep reading to gather ideas that will help you design a path that leads you to where you want to go.

Music career-driven individuals have more options than ever before and finding success - whatever you define that to be - is much easier than it once was. This chapter explores how your dreams have more opportunities for becoming a reality than you may realize.

Many people start their interest in music by playing an instrument. This experience introduces you to the basics of music and the joy of creativity, even if you don't know where that road will lead you. Obviously, if you excel at an instrument, then a career as an instrumentalist may be just what you should focus on!

But, as you look at all the professions listed, ask yourself if what excites you about music, *and* what you're skilled at, might intersect to make you a great candidate for areas you may not have thought of.

For example:
> - If you are great at debating, maybe your music calling is as a music lobbyist or copyright law/intellectual property attorney.
> - If you're already using music production software such as Pro-Tools, Logic or Ableton, you're already in the music editor/producer space.
> - If you love working with people, music therapy may be your specialty.
> - If you're good at expressing yourself in writing, could music journalism, critic, blogger or author be an avenue to explore?

The following is an extensive list, but I assure you that as comprehensive as it is, many careers are not listed. It's intended to act as a prompt to what may interest you, or you can dig a little deeper (or "riff", as musicians call it) on a theme. You may even develop hybrids of these professions or identify new opportunities. As you might expect, some careers require tremendous music knowledge or ability, while others do not.

Many of these professions also exist internationally, both remotely and in-person, so be sure to think globally as you explore! And if you're in a position to intern, many of these professions offer legitimate intern opportunities for you to explore your interest while gaining clarity on your goals. Just ensure the internship is legitimate, rather than people looking for free laborers.

For every experience music provides, there are surprising professions that are part of the process of bringing it to your ears. As an example, just watching the credits at the end of any movie, or the credits attributed to your favorite artist's recording, gives you a taste of all the talent that goes into making those final products.

> "Choose a job you love and you will never have to work a day in your life."
> -Confucius

There is the right place – and space - for you, and anyone who wants to be in music.

Let's find you your gig!

- ☐ Acoustician
- ☐ Audio engineer/scoring/mixing/remixer
    - ☐ film/TV studio
    - ☐ independent
    - ☐ radio
    - ☐ live/touring
    - ☐ performing arts theater/center
    - ☐ remote recording
    - ☐ mastering
- ☐ DJ
    - ☐ club/bar/restaurant
    - ☐ festivals/raves
    - ☐ mobile/private event/wedding
    - ☐ radio
- ☐ Instrument
    - ☐ craftsman/builder/designer
    - ☐ product demonstrator
    - ☐ sales
    - ☐ repair
    - ☐ manufactures industry representative/artist liaison
- ☐ Instrumentalist
    - ☐ casuals (private events, hotel lobbies, etc.)
    - ☐ orchestras
    - ☐ studio
    - ☐ theater (pit)
    - ☐ solo artist
    - ☐ sideman/women
    - ☐ sideline (on camera film/TV)
    - ☐ street (busker)
- ☐ Lobbyist/advocate (national/state/local)
- ☐ Mental health professional (for musicians and those in the music business)
    - o psychiatrist/psychologist/therapist
    - o mindset/life coach
- ☐ Music accountant
- ☐ Music app developer

- Music administrator
  - ex.: Mr. Holland's Opus Foundation, Save The Music, MusicCares Foundation, Fender Music Foundation, Education Through Music, etc.
    - executive director
    - development (fundraising)
    - education manager
    - program director
- Music attorney
  - freelance
  - corporate
  - firm
  - film/TV studio/record company
    - contract negotiations
    - intellectual property/copyright
    - record deals
    - publishing
- Music business manager
- Music composer
  - videogame
  - podcast
  - production music
  - film/tv
  - commercials
  - trailers
  - jingles
  - Broadway
  - animation
  - virtual reality apps
  - websites
  - industrial/documentaries
- Music conference/convention/festival producer
  - ex.: NAMM, SXSW, MIDEM, Coachella, Bonnaroo, Lollapalooza, etc.
    - speaker
    - organizer
    - educator
    - performer
    - clinician

- ☐ Music contractor
    - ☐ hotels
    - ☐ singers
    - ☐ DJs
    - ☐ musicians
    - ☐ cruise ships
    - ☐ recording sessions
- ☐ Music director and/or conductor
    - ☐ Broadway
    - ☐ touring (symphonic orchestras, musicals, artists)
    - ☐ cruise ships
    - ☐ community orchestras
    - ☐ college
    - ☐ religious
    - ☐ choral
    - ☐ orchestra (permanent or guest)
- ☐ Music director (programming/placement)
    - ☐ Spotify/Pandora/YouTube/Amazon/Deezer/iHeart Radio, etc.
    - ☐ Production music libraries (Extreme Music/UPM/APM, etc.)
    - ☐ terrestrial/satellite radio
    - ☐ podcasts
    - ☐ television shows: - (i.e., Austin City Limits, The Voice, late night TV)
- ☐ Music editor (staff or independent)
- ☐ Music educator
    - ☐ elementary
    - ☐ junior high
    - ☐ high school
    - ☐ college
    - ☐ private – individual instrumental/vocal (online or in-person)
    - ☐ private music school
    - ☐ non-profit after school music programs
- ☐ Music journalist/critic/blogger/influencer
- ☐ Music librarian
    - ☐ orchestra
    - ☐ college
- ☐ Music licensing
    - ☐ in-house (i.e., motion picture/TV studio)
    - ☐ freelance
    - ☐ private company

- Music manager/artist liaison/agent
  - representing:
    - composers
    - songwriters
    - producers
    - bands
    - artists
    - vocalists
- Music marketing/public relations/publicist
- Music merchandiser/retailer
  - online (including music memorabilia/posters)
  - brick & mortar – owner (new/used)
    - music equipment rental (backline, studio instrument rentals)
- Music museums
  - ex.: Musical Instrument Museum, Grammy Museum, Experience Music Project, Rock and Roll Museum, etc.
    - artist relations
    - curator
    - director of guest experiences
    - executive director
- Music photographer/documentarian
- Music placement companies
  - ex., Artlist, Taxi, Music Vine, etc.
    - A&R
    - owner
- Music preparation (copyist)
- Music producer
  - record/song
  - mixer/remixer
  - beat maker
- Music royalty administrator
  - record label
  - motion picture/TV Studio
  - performance rights society
  - independent
- Music supervisor
  - in-house, freelance
    - film/TV
    - advertising agency
    - theme parks
- Music venue owner/manager/booker
- Musicologist (freelance/educator)

- ☐ Orchestrator/arranger
- ☐ Performing rights organizations (employee)
  - ☐ ASCAP
  - ☐ BMI
  - ☐ SESAC
  - ☐ SoundExchange
  - ☐ Harry Fox Agency
  - ☐ international (SOCAN, SACEM, JASRAC)
- ☐ Piano tuner
- ☐ Production music companies (formerly known as library music houses)
  - o ex.: Universal Publishing Production Music, APM, KPM, Extreme Music
    - ☐ music director/supervisor
    - ☐ creative development representative
    - ☐ publishing operations manager
- ☐ Publishing
  - ☐ Sheet music publishers
    - o ex.: Hal Leonard, Alfred Music, Boosey & Hawkes
  - ☐ Song music publishers (major)
    - o ex.: Sony Music Publishing, Warner Music Publishing, BMG Music Publishing, etc.
  - ☐ Song music publishers (independent)
    - o ex.: Wixen Music, Pen Music, Kobalt Music, Downtown Music Publishing, Ditto Music Publishing, etc.
      - o jobs at the above companies include:
        - o administrator, royalty analyst, creative director, A&R, copyright, catalog manager, licensing, business affairs, etc.
- ☐ Record label
  - ☐ Artist & Repertoire (A&R)
  - ☐ music agent
  - ☐ publicist
  - ☐ promotions assistant
  - ☐ human resources associate
  - ☐ market researcher
  - ☐ creative consultant
  - ☐ marketing manager
  - ☐ owner

Music Gigs-A-Plenty

- Recording studio
    - technician/maintenance
    - owner
    - management
        - private
        - motion picture studio
- Rehearsal studio owner
- Songwriter/lyricist (countless opportunities connected to:)
    - children/animation
    - musical theater
    - librettos
    - collaborator with artists/songwriters, composers etc.
- Vocalist
    - opera
    - studio (film/TV/jingles/demos, etc.)
    - live performing (soloist/background)

Delete Your Plan "B"

What's your backup plan if you can't make it in music? Is it really sensible to go into the musical arts? Have you ever been asked these questions? Have you ever asked them of yourself? If not, you probably will.

I think a lot of the uncertainty in those questions is a lack of knowledge about the available opportunities within the music ecosystem. It seems that anyone who pursues music is inevitably asked at some point what they will do if it "doesn't work out."

People don't seem to ask those that aspire to be an attorney or doctor what *their* Plan B is if they are not successful at it, or just not very good at it, or are just unfulfilled by what the profession brings them. While the questions to future attorneys and doctors may be as simple as "Do you want to have a private practice?" or "What will your specialty be?", people unfamiliar with the arts aren't quite sure what questions to ask someone considering a music career.

Of course, a career in music can seem "iffier" because, outside of traditional employment opportunities, many people struggle to identify with the profession's uncertainty. They know intuitively that a dentist can hang out their own shingle, and their services will be perceived as required; but what does a career in music look like?

Should I only consider music a hobby while I seek out professions that assure me a steady income and security for whatever future I envision for myself, or is it part of my DNA that hungers to be fed? I admit that's a bit dramatic, but many people feel divinely (or spiritually) driven by music.

In other words, "What's your plan B"? Personally, I'm not opposed to the concept of a Plan B. Maybe it's the name that doesn't work for me because it implies that it must be one or the other. Yes, I want to be in music, but if it doesn't work out, I'll do something that isn't in music.

But how do you prepare for a successful Plan B without redirecting significant mental bandwidth away from Plan A?

Here's a thought:
What if you think of Plan B as subcategories of Plan A, but still within music - essentially a Plan A1, Plan A2, or Plan A3?

As a frequent guest speaker, I often shared my view regarding going into music full-time, saying "If you have a choice, choose something different." My intention was to suggest that the profession is so filled with talented people who are completely immersed and committed to a life in the musical arts that others who don't feel as strongly might consider looking into a career that is perceived as more stable. However, after a successful career, I think the recommendation was probably a bit elitist. Doesn't every profession have people at all skill levels who find fulfillment in their respective fields without it having to be "all or nothing?"

Fortunately, you now have the Music Gigs-A-Plenty chapter to ponder jobs you may never have known existed.

Pick out your ideal Plan A and enjoy considering all the subcategories that may be viable alternatives!

Big Bite-Sized Ideas
(in no particular order of importance)

The mini topics that follow are just quick reads covering some pretty cool ideas that can collectively help you prepare for success in music. Enjoy!

What's Your Elevator Pitch?

Have you ever heard of the *elevator pitch*? It refers to when you have only a few moments to tell someone about your talent, goals, expertise, creations or whatever. How compelling are the words that you use? How articulate and confident are you at telling people who you are and what the future is that you want? After the moment has passed, do you ask yourself, "Why didn't I say this or that?"

Like anything else, you have to practice getting good at it. Find those choice descriptors that differentiate you, that you can recall when you're in the proverbial elevator and you have only a few floors to say what you really want to say. Maybe think of yourself in the 3rd person - as a brand. Would people be interested in your product based on how you describe it?

You might want to check out the words in the Powerwords chapter for some impactful ideas.

Your Word Matters

Just like you don't want to practice bad habits when you're learning an instrument, you don't want to practice bad habits regarding your responsibility to others who are counting on you. It's one of the easiest and most important lessons to learn.

Just do what you say you're going to do, or let the person - or people - know you cannot fulfill your promise.

A specific example is just making sure you show up on time when you say you will be somewhere. It sounds so basic, and yes, sometimes you may be early, *but* being late leaves a much different impression. Next time someone makes you wait, mentally note how it feels. Regardless of what part of the music ecosystem you're in, you will most likely remember the people who show up late versus those who are on time. In a professional setting, I assure you the impact is significant, and being counted on to show up both physically and mentally is what you want people to remember. It's really about having respect for other people and recognizing that their time is as valuable to them as yours is to you. You'd be amazed at how many musicians have lost their gigs just by being late.

In the Los Angeles film/TV studio recording world, a *downbeat* time is given – the exact time that a recording session will begin. It's elementary: you're either sitting where you're supposed to be precisely when the downbeat is called, or you don't get called again. There are too many great musicians who want to be there, and making other people wait – at someone else's expense – is just not tolerated. Yes, sometimes the unexpected happens, but anticipating the unexpected is part of being a professional, regardless of what area of music you end up in.

Good things happen when people know they can trust your word, and it will benefit you in every aspect of your life.

Is That Really The Problem?

Every day we are presented with problems to solve. And while they range from tiny and insignificant to very large and impactful, sometimes you must ask yourself if you're trying to solve the *right* problem, especially if the result you're seeking seems elusive.

Making the point in a humorous way:
I stood and watched as a music director friend, who could see the keys in his ignition, frantically using a coat hanger to try and lift the inside door lock from outside his car to get into his vehicle. The problem, however, was that he neglected to first try the door handle to make sure it was locked – which it wasn't. His first question should have been whether the door was even locked, rather than assuming it was and trying to solve a problem that didn't exist.

As you look at the challenges your career goals reveal, be sure to take a hard look at whether you are purposely or inadvertently working on solving, or overcoming, the wrong obstacle.

Don't Sweat the Small Stuff

It's tough not to get aggravated when you're in an aggravating moment. But think about past moments when the challenge at hand seemed monumental. Do you look back at it now through the same lens as when it happened? Maybe. But I bet most people will say it seemed like a bigger deal at the time, or things just eventually worked out.

Not to minimize how important it feels in the moment, but in retrospect, asking how much *it* will matter in a day, month or year can help keep things in perspective.

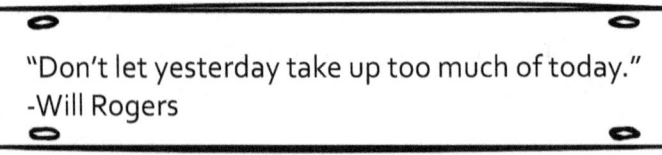

"Don't let yesterday take up too much of today."
-Will Rogers

Scan The Environment

I once had the pleasure to lunch with a drummer who greatly influenced my early professional drumming years. While his musicianship was very respected within the business, he felt that the biggest reason for the decline in his career was his resistance to embracing emerging technology. He believed that the demand would always be there for a solely acoustic drummer, and as he stood his ground, adapting drummers got the work he wanted. He eventually had to settle for the leftover gigs.

The moral of the story?: Stay informed on all trends, track where they've come from and where you think they're heading, and ask smart questions on how your skill set can remain relevant and valuable as the world changes.

Disrupters and futurists appear in everyone's lifetime. Just look at the transformation in the distribution of the recorded music industry by companies such as CD Baby and TuneCore, and by streaming services such as Spotify and Amazon Music. Of course, it isn't just music: eBay, Uber, Crypto, AI, NFTs... and the list grows daily.

As the barriers-to-entry in all aspects of the music industry continues to lower, always be prepared! Tomorrow's companies are looking to gain a competitive advantage by looking into the future today. Are you?

Ask. Ask. And Ask Some More

There is power in asking questions and never underestimating the impact of showing curiosity in another person's world. People naturally enjoy people who are genuinely listening to them, and you'll usually learn more than you expect if you take the time to be inquisitive. And if you're shy, asking questions can help you open up to another person while making you feel more comfortable.

On the other hand, I used to marvel at people who would meet with me only to hear themselves talk about unrelated topics. The meetings were inevitably short and unfruitful, so that's just something to consider if you feel you may be prone to doing that (which many of us are).

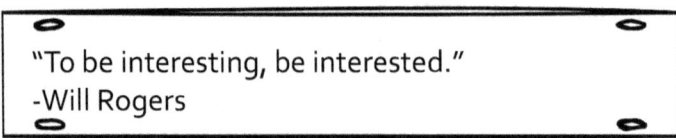

"To be interesting, be interested."
-Will Rogers

Writer Dale Carnegie said, "You can make more friends in two months by becoming interested in other people than you can in two years by trying to get other people interested in you."

Choose Your Battles Wisely

The phrase "choose your battles wisely" has been said for eons. I interpret it to mean that there are some fights (metaphorically speaking) worth being passionate about. And then there are those that are just better to walk away from.

Only you can decide how you want to react to something.

A quote I like from motivational speaker Richard Carlson says, "If someone throws you the ball, you don't have to catch it."

To Make It Real – Speak Up

Talk to enough people and you will find that, without exception, they consider their success to have come from consistently putting themselves out there to plant seeds that might someday grow. However, without that effort you can hardly expect people to know what you want. Opportunities can appear where and when you least expect them because you believe enough in yourself to let others know your dreams.

A more Zen thought might be that whatever future you envision already exists. It's up to you to decide what paths you'll choose to get there.

Just verbally sharing your long-term goals or short-term deadlines can make you feel more accountable to achieving your goals - especially when telling them to someone you don't want to let down.

> "You don't have to see the whole staircase, just take the first step."
> -Martin Luther King, Jr

Putting your ambitions in print can also be effective.

Very early on in my career, I tried something called visualization. I must have been taking a moment to daydream when I put myself in my own contact list with the title of Senior Vice-President, Music. There was no reason to expect that to be in my future, but I liked the idea of seeing it in writing whenever I looked through my contact list. It came true.

What part of your future would you like to see in writing today?

"Decompose" Yourself

Sometimes, the problem is so big or complex that we don't know where to start.

Unless you practice *decomposition* - the idea that significant challenges are more likely to be overcome if they are reduced to smaller pieces. It's powerful and effective.

If you play an instrument and are having a problem with a particular bar or bars of music, it's a common recommendation to slow down the tempo, take it in small increments beat-by-beat, and build from there. What if you applied that to your music career goals? Take what seems like a big decision and break it into an arbitrary number of "buckets"; *then* solve the challenge that each one of those buckets holds.

Eventually, that challenge will no longer be what it was.

Be A Kid at Any Age

Pablo Picasso said, "Every child is an artist." The challenge is how to remain an artist once we grow up. When we are young, our ideas and expressions flow freely, unfiltered, and without self-criticism. As we age, holding onto that spirit can become elusive, unless we recognize that our inner child is always within us to tap at will. Whether as an instrumentalist, songwriter, or with any career focus, don't forget to use your playful creativity and sense of wonder to open new avenues or to create new ideas.

Curiosity can be invigorating, and asking "how" or "why" may lead you to unexpected and welcomed innovations in your music career objectives.

Don't deny yourself the thrill of exploration!

Success Is Effort

The huge block letter sign above my music teacher's blackboard read, "Success is the result of effort." That banner announced during every lesson that if I wanted to be good at my music, I might need to put in some effort. I know now how very true that statement was. Still, I believe it needs a bit of modification to read that "Success is the result of *consistent* effort." If you just put the time in, the result may not always be successful, but if you set out realistic goals and diligently strive to reach those goals, there's a much better chance of arriving at your desired destination.

And while most people in music never have stratospheric success, those who persevere find their niche more often than not.

Thomas Alva Edison is undoubtedly one of the world's most prolific inventors. His 1,093 patents include the phonograph, the motion picture camera and, of course, the light bulb. Edison tried 2,774 different materials in search of a filament for the light bulb. When a reporter asked, "How did it feel to fail so many times?", Edison replied, "I didn't fail 2,774 times. The light bulb was an invention with 2,774 steps".

> "Success doesn't come from what you do occasionally. It comes from what you do consistently."
> -Marie Foleo

And what about success versus fame?

Success can come in many forms, arrive in small or large doses, be applauded by many or by few, and often shows up after incremental accomplishments. And while fame equals recognition and potentially money, does it equal success and happiness? Many famous people question whether they have succeeded based on their personal view of success, which may differ considerably from public perception.

Be Prepared

If you read the chapter towards the end of this book entitled "The Whole Story", you may notice that on several occasions I did some extensive research about the people I planned on meeting with who I knew could be helpful in my career goals. Not just about their professional path but also about the projects they or their companies had done, and especially the ones they were in the middle of. Most importantly, I looked for intersections between the skills I possessed and how they could be of benefit to what they were currently working on.

I was fortunate that doing so came to me instinctively, but I know it's not as natural for many. The people I have been most impressed with, and have looked forward to working with, are those that did some homework to show their interest in what we'd be meeting about. On the other hand, for example, I have met with composers who would play me music 180 degrees from anything I'd ever need, or offer a service that had no connection to any project I was working on and likely would never need in the future.

If you're serious about wanting a positive outcome, try to put yourself in the other person's position to figure out what might pique their interest in what you have to offer. It can sometimes be challenging to assess, but it's definitely worth the effort and it might just differentiate you from others.

WHOA... Wait A Second

Fight the urge to be critical before it's warranted. Maybe a better way to say it is: fight the urge to be instantly dissatisfied.

Our instinct is to self-edit as soon as we bring forward an idea - before it can breathe and be looked at from different angles.

Why do that?

Get it on paper, in a conversation, on a recording or on your computer to make it real - and then return to it later. It may not be as valuable as you had hoped, but then again, it may have much more "shine" on it than you first imagined.

In addition, your subconscious brain has a habit of continuing to work on things in the background, which is why sometimes something you can't remember just pops into your head unexpectedly long after you were first trying to remember it. You may find that, in the interim, your creative juices developed new ideas or perspectives while you were engaged in other activities.

I Love Music, But I'm Not That Creative

Relax! You <u>are</u> creative. We are all creative. It's all about how you define it. When people say that they don't *think* they're creative, they are usually referring to those who write music, poetry, scriptwriting, painting, singing, cooking, woodworking – things that people generally see as a creative art with a tangible or aural result. But throughout the day you use creativity to navigate the world, formulate thoughts to convey your thinking, or devise new ways to improve productivity or happiness.

I remember dreading a class I had to take on statistics. I knew it would be very dull, and dealing with numbers and data analysis would probably put me to sleep. Imagine my surprise when my teacher welcomed us all to a class on creativity! Her introduction piqued my interest as she explained that while numbers have finite values, how we manipulate them can be very creative. She went on to talk about how algorithms, formulas, etc., are all part of a creative process before they prove themselves useful as parts of the daily products we all rely upon.

While mathematics and statistics may be on the other side of the average person's response to the question "What is creative?", I continue to look at the world around me and every profession listed in the Music Gigs-A-Plenty chapter as falling into the realm of creativity.

Time Travel

Don't hesitate to imagine the future as you want it to be. Fast-forward in your mind one week, month, year and decade. Take your time and picture what you want to see - or employ "stretch goals" to envision beyond what you hope to accomplish.

It's your future – make it what you want it to be. And when you return to the current moment's reality, think about what path might take you to the dream you imagined.

> "You can't change yesterday, but you have today to make the changes you want for your tomorrow."
> -Anonymous

Bring It Into Focus

The saying goes, "Focus on your strengths, not your weaknesses." The message implies that, by doing so, you will gain confidence and positive momentum as that strength becomes stronger. However, what are now your strengths were most likely once your weaknesses, so maybe the saying should flip and say, "Focus <u>proportionately</u> on your weaknesses <u>and</u> your strengths."

Low-hanging fruit is the term used for things in life that are easily accessible. That's not a bad thing at all - at the right time. I have lots of familiar drum fills I love using that will always turn out well. But what about those fills I have yet to work on or have heard other drummers play that blow me away?

I know it will take some serious practicing before I can play them, but relying on what always works isn't what growth is all about — it's about turning what used to be weaknesses into strengths.

Be (somewhat) Pushy

A prominent theme throughout this book is persistence. And with 27,000 music degrees awarded yearly in the U.S. - on top of anyone's guess of how many non-college-bound people commit to going into a music career) - persistence is an attribute.

However, it is also a bit of an art form.

And while personal persistence, or drive, is an attribute, professional persistence comes with a fine line between being persistent, annoying or even obnoxious. Try to read between the lines to gauge what level of persistence will pay off and what may offend. Not sure? Always ease up rather than push harder, since once you cross the line it's tough to go back.

The art form part of this is knowing where the line is before you cross it. It comes down to being intuitive and reading the signs. What is the person's tone of voice, physical movements, and/or words via texts or emails *really* saying?

Having met many composers and musicians looking for work, I can attest to the unintended reactions to talented people who push inappropriately hard.

> "A black belt is a white belt who never quit."
> -Anonymous

First Impressions DO Matter

No matter who you are, you never get a second chance to make a first impression.

Be who you are. Be authentic. But know your audience. Being naïve by believing first impressions don't matter doesn't prevent other people from having first impressions of you.

If dressing in a specific way makes sense, dress for the situation and *then* modify your future choices if it calls for it, but try and "read the room" the best you can beforehand. Some people call it having "perceptive situational awareness." Regardless of what *"the room"* is, there is always something (or someone) to guide you in making whatever impression you want to make.

Use meaningful eye contact *if* you think it will lend more sincerity, or avoid it entirely if you feel the opposite. Maybe a handshake is more appropriate than a fist bump, or perhaps a nod does the trick? And lastly, although it may seem obvious, the use of "please" and "thank you" are still appropriate responses that can convey sincerity and appreciation at the right moment.

Remember that all the small things add up.

Play, Play, And Play Some More

As an instrumentalist (and this applies to songwriting, producing, remixing, etc.), grab any chance to play/collaborate with people in any setting possible.

When you make music with other people, you're on a different "plane" where non-verbal communication occurs. But, just like any learned language, it must be practiced and refined. If you're an instrumentalist: Does your school have a wind ensemble? marching band? musical theater? If you're beyond that point, play gigs such as private events, parties, bars, clubs, or coffeehouses wherever, and whenever possible. And don't be shy when open mic nights are available.

The more experience you have interacting with other musicians - this includes jamming, virtual collaborating, or any other form of informal music-making - the more you'll increase your musical vocabulary.

And while it's commonplace to work in a digital audio workstation environment where tracks are electronically created and sent to others, it provides a very different experience when you are in *real-time* with other musicians.

It's all about finding the right balance.

And how can this concept apply to the music entrepreneur not in the music performance/production "arena"? Simple. Whatever your interest is, there are other like-minded people who you can benefit from and who can benefit from you. Consider creating your own in-person network with people who can meet to discuss current trends, ideas and future goals. And don't forget to read the chapter "You Are Not Alone" to connect with professional organizations that may be applicable to your interest.

Running Dry On Ideas

Do you ever feel like you've run out of ideas? Not just musical ideas but anything for which you might need a new idea? The solution is simple: don't keep looking in the same place for your new idea or inspiration unless you want to keep getting the same results.

I once used a phone book – yes, one of those free directories that used to show up at your front door – to randomly find companies that might need a jingle written for them. I'd call them and ask if they ever needed a customized song for their business. The truth is, I never got a gig that way, *but* it gave me the idea to create personalized songs for special occasions. I made $1000's writing simple and entertaining songs, and I got a lot of media attention for doing so, including the front page of the *Los Angeles Times'* People section and a long segment on a popular TV show. It was never intended to be a long-term career, but it filled the gap.

Look and listen at seemingly unrelated events and discover connections you may not have thought of. For example: when you hear the sound of your washing machine, does the rhythm create a "groove" in your mind that could be the basis for a new song? When you watch credits on a television or movie, what job titles intrigue you, and how might they intersect with your career interests/goals? When you discover new websites, do you question what role, if any, your talent might be able to play in helping them succeed?

The colors in a prism don't change unless you change your angle or the angle of the prism. You might find an unexpected spark if you look elsewhere – especially in unlikely places.

Embrace The Gray Zone!

Things aren't always black and white. Uncertainty even has its own acronym these days called VUCA - the states of volatility, uncertainty, complexity, and ambiguity. But what about learning to thrive in the moment when that's precisely how it is? Some stock market moguls love waiting for VUCA moments to strategically turn that environment in their favor. While not an easy place to be, trying to turn those insecure moments into something positive means you're primed to come out ahead.

Stay focused on what's *really* important, be creative navigating those times, and trust yourself to get through it.

> "Whether you think you can or you think you can't, you're right."
> -Henry Ford

You're Already Skilled

Whether you're a student or not, don't undervalue the skills you already have. In other words, don't underestimate your strengths and the competencies you show the world every day. Even if it's not music-related, attributes such as determination and initiative are always well-received by prospective collaborators, employers, etc. As an example, successfully completing school or work projects means you've demonstrated how to commit, display follow-through, and work with people; donating to a charity, which shows empathy – a foundational necessity for becoming a music therapist; or the ability to engage, entertain and convey ideas is foundational gold for an inspirational educator and for self-marketing.

From getting a driver's license or using critical thinking to solve problems, you have more skills than you may realize that can apply to your career choice - if you recognize the similarities.

Challenge The Rules

Don't forget to challenge the status quo or the supposed musical rules. Musical counterpoint began in the Middle Ages, but as I studied the extensive rules that developed for this form of composing, I realized that this is precisely what inspired new forms of musical expression to subsequently emerge. Creative people have an inborn urge to push the envelope and explore new possibilities by breaking the rules, which you can hear by following the evolution of music over the centuries.

This thinking can also apply to any career objective you're trying to achieve. Natural instincts guide you to the path of least resistance but may not lead you to the path of greatest success. Metaphorically speaking, any house you're trying to enter has multiple entry points, with the front door being the most obvious. While many people will stop when the front door is locked, don't forget to try the window, the chimney, the side door, etc., to gain access to the information, opportunities or results you seek.

Have you ever heard of the word "moxie"? If not (but you have it), you don't let a minor setback stop you from trying again because you're a determined person who doesn't give up easily.

Where are you on the moxie meter?

How Does Your Gut Feel

Listen to your "gut" – which some people call a "hunch," "intuition" or a "sixth sense." We are the sum of all our experiences, and our brain records it all. Although we obviously can't access all our memories, our so-called "instincts" pull from our conscious and unconscious database to communicate a path that feels right - and often safe - for us.

Listening to that voice can often guide us in making unexpected choices, even when they don't feel completely rational. *Listening*, of course, doesn't suggest *obeying*, but it is another tool in your mental toolbox to guide you.

Be A Realistic Optimist

I recall being hired for a recording session by a producer demoing a song he had hoped would be a massive success for his singer. The session went very well, and while we were all celebrating the song in the studio, he turned to me and said I'd be the first drummer he'd call from now on.

He never called me again.

While his comment may have been 100% sincere, he may have subsequently encountered other unexpected challenges and/or disappointments and was a reminder to me that life happens to other people, too.

Aim high: enjoy the moment, and the compliment if it comes, and be optimistic. This doesn't mean you can't simultaneously be realistic, but optimism feels good and generates positivity.

And, very simply, people like to be around positive people.

It's All Been Written Before

A friend once said, "I don't think I have any more notes in me; it feels like it's all been written before." He then went on to write as much music as 40 Beethoven symphonies.

Think about the 26 letters in the English alphabet. That's all there are! Go into the biggest bookstore or library in the (English-speaking) world; every word in every book is just a combination of those 26 letters. That means, since millions of books get published yearly, an infinite combination of those letters creates new thoughts and stories. Yes, this is an obvious and simplistic idea, but music is no different.

There are 12 notes in our familiar octave. That's it. Yes, there are multiple octaves, but only 12 notes. How many compositions have been created with the use of those 12 notes? Billions, maybe? That means *you* have a palate to mix and create, as if it's the first time your creation has been created. Like a painter, there may be combinations of colors and styles similar to what has come before, but *you* are unique, and therefore so are your choices! Fortunately, today's digital palate is greater than ever, giving you more options than at any other time in history.

You are the only one to see the world through your lens, and your voice (or whatever vehicle you use to communicate) is truly unique on this planet.

Even though more than 75,000 songs are uploaded daily to streaming services, and AI-assisted composing (or even unassisted composing) may reshape the way music is created, *you* can always bring something to the table that no one else can. This is because your creativity, and even your imperfections, are solely yours!

> "When you have exhausted all possibilities, remember this—you haven't."
> -Thomas Edison

Put Me In The Zone

I remember conversing with a renowned musician with 30 Grammy awards to his name about the magic of making music *in the zone* (a natural euphoric connection with the musicians you're playing with when it feels like you could almost leave your body in an altered state of consciousness and the music would continue on this "cosmic plane" all by itself). Once you've experienced it, it's a very positive addiction you look forward to having again.

What was especially interesting about our conversation was his suggestion that the feeling doesn't have to be limited to just musicians interacting with one another.

Even if you haven't had a euphoric musical experience, think about the moments you may have had. It might have been when playing a sport, giving a presentation, trying to articulate a complex thought, or finishing a rehearsal that felt inspired. Think about what came together to provide you with that feeling. Was it your mood, a good night's sleep, preparedness, or something someone said to you? This is just something to think about, since repeating those moments can elevate motivation, self-confidence and produce creativity.

May Luck Be With You

Many have told me that I've been very lucky in my career. Have I been? Did I sit around and wait for luck to call me in upstate New York and invite me to Los Angeles? The answer is no. But I did make choices that helped luck find its way to me more easily.

Luck, as defined by the Roman philosopher Seneca, is "the intersection of preparedness and opportunity." I immediately identified with that definition as a more precise explanation of what "luck" really is. While buying a winning lottery ticket might be called pure luck - meaning you won because of a completely random act of the stars aligning - you can help make professional luck a bit less random.

Every so often, luck really is all in the timing. Some call it serendipity or synchronicity - when a happy accident, fluke, or unexpected good fortune occurs. And sometimes you're in situations with more potential for luck to emerge. One thing is clear though: nothing will happen if you haven't made the effort to put yourself "out there" in the first place. And to do that involves another developmental skill: risk.

Everyone has their own degree of risk tolerance, depending on what's involved, but the familiar phrase that there is *no reward without risk* is not without merit. You may also find that others see people who take risks as having the admirable trait of courage.

Allowing yourself the freedom to take risks - and possibly fail, or, as I prefer to think of it, find success through a different approach - is an invitation for opportunity to present itself to you.

The phrase "carpe diem" (the Latin term for "seize the day") is a popular and powerful one. It serves as an excellent motto to suggest that taking action and showing up for life's possibilities, known and unexpected, creates better odds than waiting for them to come to you.

> "If you want more luck, take more chances."
> -Brian Tracy

So, if one definition of luck is "the intersection of preparedness and opportunity", and opportunity has presented itself (via luck, synchronicity, serendipity or whatever), the other side of the luck coin is preparedness. And if you haven't done all you can to prepare yourself for that moment, then that lucky moment may come and go without value.

Of course, since you are forever preparing for what life throws at you, who knows when you'll be completely prepared for what comes your way. However, learning life skills and the details of your career objectives are all part of the preparation to be as ready as possible.

And that's what this book is all about!

> "The harder I work, the luckier I get."
> -Coleman Cox

Positivity

A play on a familiar proverb says, "as you think, so you are." While wildly open to interpretation, it seems logical that positive things can happen if you think positively. The inverse of that seems even more apparent and is a slippery slope that's much harder to climb up from. It's easy to forget that you can't control how others think, but you can always be authentic to yourself.

Negative assumptions or, as I like to call them, dream killers, assume the negative. After that, it's a quick leap to finding thoughts that validate that assumption. I guess the question is, why wouldn't you try to eliminate the assumption rather than censoring the dream?

Have you ever heard of an affirmation? Well, it's like a shot of positivity filled with the exact words you want to hear - said by you, to you – whenever you want or need it! It's a gift/reward you can give yourself that's always in your back pocket. Concise, memorable sentences (or possibly just one sentence) usually starting with "I" and using words that actualize how you want to see yourself and your future, are effective.

> "Your mind is a powerful thing. When you fill it with positive thoughts, your life will start to change."
> -Coleman Cox

Experiment with what parts of your affirmations resonate, and adjust as needed. You can also make affirmations for different aspects of your life to say at different times of the day.

Consistency in when and where you practice your affirmation (verbally, mentally, or written) will also aid your subconscious in letting the thoughts sink in. First thing in the morning? Last thing at night? Before practicing? Before challenging moments?

You may find that the benefits of increased self-esteem and self-confidence are evident in your motivation, relationships, musical performance, mental and physical health, and how you navigate your music career goals. Sounds pretty good, huh?!

There are many internet resources for affirmations, but here are a few examples of mine that I like to use:

> - I believe in myself and my music.
> - I know there is a place for me in the music industry, and I'm worthy of finding it.
> - I pursue my passion for music with honesty and integrity.
> - I will block out negative thinking and surround myself with positive people.
> - I am enough and acknowledge my self-worth.
> - I trust in my talent and creativity.
> - I am exceptional at being my best self.
> - I fulfill my dreams through persistence and passion.
> - I am confident and strong.
> - I am courageous enough to have a successful music career.
> - My optimism and confidence create determination.
> - I will succeed while maintaining humility, heart and honesty.
> - My love for the music industry is infectious and sincere.
> - I am proud of my ambition.
> - The world and people around me inspire my creativity.

> I can accomplish anything I set my mind to.
> I am mindful of my physical and mental health to achieve my dreams.

> "If you don't like something, change it. If you can't change it, change your attitude."
> -Maya Angelou

Check out the Powerwords chapter for some word ideas, but the most important thing is that the affirmation speaks to you in your voice and is easy to say repetitively.

Top Secret - For Your Mind Only

In our quiet moments, we can ask ourselves anything we want and be pretty honest with our answers because, after all, we are the only ones who will hear our responses.

Ask yourself the following questions *or* whatever similar questions are meaningful to you, and allow yourself the vulnerability of answering honestly.

> - What do I perceive "good enough" to mean?
> - Why do I want what I want?
> - How competitive am I?
> - Am I concerned with competition?
> - What is at stake and how will I feel if I don't achieve my goals?
> - Why do I want a career in music?

- What does success really mean to me? Money? Happiness? Respect? In what order and to what degree?
- Do I fear failure? Do I fear success?
- What do I think must happen for me to be successful?
- What does true success mean to me?
- Do I self-sabotage?
- How risk-tolerant am I?
- What do I like most and least about considering a career in music?
- How long am I anticipating my chosen field to be in demand?
- Am I surrounding myself with positive people who support, motivate and inspire me?
- Am I self-disciplined?
- Am I self-confident?

Powerwords

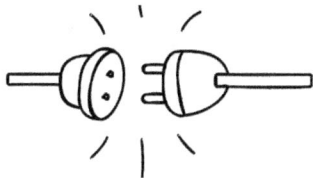

Confucius said, "You are as you think." So, with that in mind...

I am a bit of a word junkie (something you probably don't hear every day).

Over the years, I have been intrigued by the words people use to convey their ideas powerfully or emotionally. How you think of yourself and the words you use to describe yourself, your music and your music career goals can help shape your reality. They can also be springboards to other ideas for you and your music goals.

DO	HAVE	BE
achieve	self-discipline	engaged
differentiate	confidence	passionate
dream	curiosity	resilient
visualize	heart	focused
explore	perseverance	optimistic
improve	ambition	innovative
take risks	initiative	intuitive
	integrity	inspired
	imagination	proactive
	authenticity	trustworthy
	momentum	unlimited
	determination	persistent
	endurance	fearless
		motivated
		energized
		strategic
		credible

Even if none of these words is your style, what are the words you use to communicate your ideas and thoughts to yourself and the people around you?

Thick Skin

A career in the arts, whether music or any other artistic form of expression, takes courage and a commitment to succeed against what may seem like bigger odds than more "traditional," "sensible" or "safe" professions.

We all have ups and downs and times of self-doubt, making it hard to push forward. Of course, some people experience that more than others, and there are as many points on that scale as there are people.

Do people who find careers in music experience more of those emotional swings than other professions? Maybe. But the question is, do you? Or will you?

All things being equal, some careers have more perceived stability and are much less subjective to outside opinions. An example of extremes may be that of an elementary music schoolteacher and a freelance musician. One gets a weekly paycheck and validation from students and administration, versus a freelance career with seemingly unlimited variables.

When considering a career in music, an obvious question is, "Am I good enough?". And a good follow-up question is, "What do I perceive *good enough* to really mean?" If I compare myself to others, am I holding myself to a comparable or unrealistic standard? If it's unrealistic, why am I being harder on myself than is rationale?

Questioning can be as healthy as it can be unhealthy; it's how we process our self-doubting that matters. And it's important to understand that sometimes things will go as planned, and other times they just won't.

Practicing how you handle rejection and criticism can help you stand on emotionally solid ground, and help weather, for example, faceless social media.

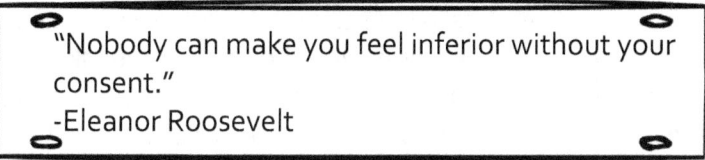

"Nobody can make you feel inferior without your consent."
-Eleanor Roosevelt

As a child, you get applauded for the smallest accomplishment. As you get older, the response becomes understandably more reserved, but our appetite for that positive reinforcement remains. When it doesn't come as expected, it's up to us to pat ourselves on the back, say we did a good job and not look to others for the validation we feel we deserve.

Do you have a fear of failure, embarrassment, rejection or even achievement? Welcome to the club! We all do this to a certain degree, and each person works in their own way to overcome the adverse effects of these emotions.

And let's not forget about the people we surround ourselves with. Have you ever noticed how much better you feel when surrounded by people who feed your self-confidence? And, conversely, how good it feels to support others who are working hard to accomplish something? If you don't get the support you need from your family, be sure to get it from others you surround yourself with.

> "I used to think anyone doing something weird was weird. Now I know it's the people that call others weird that are weird."
> -Paul McCartney

Your career goal will inevitably have hurdles to overcome. People face challenges and adversity daily, but those life experiences can be channeled into your chosen creative output. Duke Ellington said, "I merely took the energy it took to pout and wrote some blues."

And then there's dealing with criticism. Criticism can hurt, whether it comes from a friend, family or the public, where everyone always seems to have an opinion. However, the thicker your skin gets, the easier it is to ignore the impact you allow them to have on you. It's also a learning tool for choosing our words to criticize others. But, of course, constructive criticism can sometimes help us grow.

> "To avoid criticism, say nothing, do nothing, and be nothing."
> -Elbert Hubbard

One last thought. If whatever came at you is emotionally eating at you, try this tip: take out a pen and some paper – not a laptop or other electronic device – and write to the person without filtering anything you're feeling. Write why it hurt, how it affected you, and anything else that comes to mind, and when you've got it all down on paper... destroy it. You've got nothing to lose by trying it, and for some people, it can be highly cathartic!

Let's Get Motivated

One of my music mentors once gave me a very strange homework assignment. He had me read a book entitled *16 Books That Changed the World* by Robert B. Downs. It is a collection of writings that influenced the course of history, from some of the most important works ever written by authors such as Freud, Newton, Darwin, Einstein, Marx and Machiavelli. When we got to the lesson, all he wanted to talk about was what I thought of the book.

Of course, that day's real lesson was to learn that there is a world out there to learn from, and that the music we create is the output of all we have learned. By ignoring - or at least not paying much attention - to things other than music, we are cutting ourselves off from ideas, theories, etc. that can be extremely motivating and significantly affect our music *and* career outlook.

When was the last time you visited an art museum, or any non-music-related venue, to get inspiration that might help change the lens you are used to looking through every day? How about a podcast, blog or book outside your normal area of interest? The list is as endless as the creativity you have within yourself.

Be kind to yourself, and don't forget to give yourself a mental pat on the back when you've accomplished a goal. Large or small, it's easy to forget that we deserve to enjoy self-acknowledgment and pride when we've succeeded. It's much easier to be hard on yourself, but recognizing that you've made progress at any point in your journey feels great and is healthy self-motivation!

Celebrate what goes well while identifying what you can improve upon.

Believe it or not, donating your time can give you motivation from unexpected emotional places which can indirectly help your music goals – or any goal, for that matter. And, as mentioned in the Math/Schmath chapter, the act of giving can have a ripple effect, and you never know what impact your words or actions can have on someone else. Sometimes it can last a lifetime, and you'd never know you were the catalyst.

I'll Do It Tomorrow

Procrastination can be habit-forming but, like any habit, it can be modified with a behavior change. When it impedes your success, having some ideas about how to minimize it can be helpful.

Here are a few things to consider:
Write down and prioritize what you want to accomplish in a realistic amount of time for your task (or practice session) and stick to it. Start with short periods you know you can honor, and build up daily, breaking down what you're trying to accomplish into smaller, manageable parts. Then, incrementally succeed at those before taking on the entire goal, because small incremental progress adds up!

Sometimes it takes more effort or creativity to devise an excuse *not* to practice or strategize, or to make that call or email or...whatever. If you're in an environment that makes it easy to find excuses, try to change your environment. It could be as simple as going to a different location, such as a coffee shop or library, or using noise-cancelling headphones. If you're looking hard enough for a reason not to do something, you'll find it. But if you're really looking to be productive, use your creativity to find that suitable physical space.

You might also ask yourself if there is a specific reason you're putting off doing something. Are you concerned about failing, rejection or being imperfect? Does avoiding doing what you want/need to do feel safer? Only you know the real reasons you're putting something off, but it may take some honest self-questioning to figure out what the excuses may be covering up.

> "If you don't change what you are doing today, all of your tomorrows will look like yesterday."
> -Jim Rohn

Your phone is probably your biggest distraction, as it is for many of us. It's a lifeline to the world in so many ways that it makes sense we gravitate to it the way we do. The obvious challenge is when we want to focus on something else, and it's "in the wings" emitting alerts that call to us. It's difficult when we know access to the internet, email, texts and social media are within reach.

The simple solution? Power it down completely and get going with the business at hand! Hint: place the phone in another room so it's out of sight.

And when you're done, give yourself a reward. You don't have to make it a big deal but allow yourself to enjoy something that didn't take priority over what you first needed to do. An episode of your favorite show? An ice cream? A nap? *You* know better than anyone what it is that fits this description.

Standing On The Shoulders Of Others

Sir Isaac Newton wrote: "We are who we are because of the hard work of the people who came before us."

Most everything in this world has been an evolutionary process. All the products you see around you are the never-ending result of people building on the ideas that have come before them.

The wheel was invented in the 4th century B.C., and some archaeologists hypothesize that the invention happened in one place and by one person. Just look at what ideas the wheel is based upon today! Of course, the wheel alone is often ineffective unless accompanied by an axle; so even then, people were "riffing" on inventions to make new derivative works.

Music is no different. And every facet of the music business is built by people influenced and inspired by people who came before them and those currently creating. And it doesn't necessarily mean within one's own field, either. A unique idea or perspective can emerge when sparked from any medium, just as a musical artist can influence the creation of other works of art, movies or whatever.

How can Gregorian Chants from the Medieval Ages period influence you now? Or better yet, imagine how your favorite talent - dead or alive - would respond to what you're creating or how you are approaching your career goal. What would *they* suggest if you could sit down and have a conversation with them?

The following is just a small slice of talent and an arrow connecting them to people they've mentioned having been inspired by.

You may find it interesting to look into who may have influenced the people you admire.

Famous Person	→	Their Inspiration
Madonna	→	Aretha Franklin
The Beatles	→	Chuck Berry
Taylor Swift	→	Shania Twain
Led Zeppelin	→	Vanilla Fudge
Jay-Z	→	Marvin Gaye
Bad Bunny	→	Marc Anthony
Mark Zuckerberg	→	Bill Gates
Jimi Hendrix	→	Buddy Guy
The Ramones	→	The Troggs
Leonard Bernstein	→	George Gershwin
Wolfgang Amadeus Mozart	→	Franz Joseph Haydn
Notorious B.I.G.	→	Grandmaster Flash
Mariah Carey	→	Billie Holiday
Lucianna Pavarotti	→	Mario Lanza
Claude Debussy	→	Richard Wagner
Elvis Presley	→	Hank Williams

The Music Business Is The People Business

Relationships

The book you are reading highlights that the skills you need to be successful in whatever music-related field you may enter are many. However, over the years I have found one common - and obvious - similarity in the people who have attained significant levels of achievement in the music industry: they all benefitted from the ability to form healthy and sustained relationships.

These relationships, which exist on many levels simultaneously, create a lifetime *and* lifeline network. These networks yield fruit over time, but only if the ability to create meaningful relationships is developed in the first place.

We don't generally think much about how we make friends, relate to strangers, communicate our frustrations, or share our feelings. Still, the better you get at these fundamental interactions, the better you feel about yourself, creating an aura people want to be around.

Make listening, instead of talking, habitual, and you'll be amazed at the rewards. *Really* listening when people speak is much more than just hearing what they're saying. It's taking in the words, tone and body language and trying to understand what they might be feeling. It's about being present in the moment and giving that person your full attention.

> "You can make more friends in two months by becoming interested in other people than you can in two years by trying to get other people interested in you."
> -Dale Carnegie

Stay connected

This relates more to professionals you meet along the way, but how exactly do you maintain relationships with people you don't regularly spend time with? One way that has always worked for me is by looking for interesting articles or websites they may find interesting and forwarding it to them, with a brief personal note, without expecting anything in return.

But keep it short. The value of your time will always be different from someone else's, and brevity is generally a safer strategy. This is not the opportunity to talk about yourself, but about gradually building a connection.

Lastly, I will go out on a limb and say that no matter what the past or future is like (distant or otherwise), there is no better way to develop a relationship than seeing someone in person. Yes, video conversations via Facetime, or the like, are a good substitute. However, there is something inherently different about sharing the same environment which promotes a more personal conversation that can't be as easily disturbed or interrupted.

Collaboration

Being receptive to collaborating can be a *game changer*. Leaving your ego at the door and finding compatible collaborators can create the building blocks of something exceptional.

No matter who you admire, it took collaboration to produce what emerged from the creative energy each participant brought to the table.

As examples, when these duos first met, they had no idea their collaborations would inspire and impact millions of others:

> Henry Wells and William G. Fargo
> John Lennon and Paul McCartney
> Bill Gates and Paul Allen
> Steve Jobs and Steve Wozniak
> Bill Hewlett and David Packard
> William Procter and James Gamble
> Dr. Dre and Jimmy Iovine
> Richard Rodgers and Oscar Hammerstein
> Jimmy Jam and Terry Lewis
> Elton John and Bernie Taupin
> Jimmy Page and Robert Plant
> Paul Simon and Art Garfunkel
> Meriwether Lewis and William Clark

Networking

LinkedIn is brilliant at highlighting the fact that people know people who know people. It underscores that you can never underestimate how often it's just a few degrees of separation between you and someone you'd like to connect with. Even the people around you have their "orbits" of others with whom you could become future colleagues.

I recall a conversation with an entertainment industry icon who had worked with people considered the who's who of television/motion pictures and politics. As we walked, I told him how impressed I was with the people he had had the opportunity to know. He stopped our stroll and, with a slight smile, looked at me and said, "It's not about the people *you* know, it's about the people who say they know *you* that matters."

Camaraderie

During the time I was head of music at Paramount Pictures Television, there were a handful of large television production companies, which included Sony, Universal, 20th Century Fox, MGM, Disney, and Warner Bros. Each studio had significant music divisions, and everyone knew who was at the helm of each one.

Since many of our challenges were similar, the seven of us would occasionally have dinner to enjoy each other's company. While being very careful not to violate company confidentiality, we would share in ways that gave support and a deeper insight into shared experiences.

While the companies we worked for were definitely competitors, the friendships that emerged from our small group transcended that reality. Our meetings allowed us to benefit both personally and professionally by establishing mutual trust and respect.

Are there people you could become closer with that might yield positive, and potentially creative, results?

You Are Not Alone

If the internet teaches us anything, it's that we are not alone. Your ability to tap into people and professional organizations with similar interests is just a few clicks away - with many offering quite a bit of information without you having to formally join.

People involved in these organizations are already like-minded, or wouldn't be members, so reaching out to them and asking questions - especially naive ones - may lead to interesting responses you didn't expect.

I am sure there are many more destinations I haven't listed, but take the time to look through the sites, even if you think they may not be exactly what you're looking for. The sites may also give you other ideas to use as a springboard for further exploration:

ACM (Academy of Country Music)
AES (Audio Engineering Society)
ASA (Academy of Scoring Arts)
AFM (American Federation of Musicians)
AIMP (Association of Independent Music Publishers)
AMP (Association of Music Producers)
AMTA (American Music Therapy Association)
ASMAC (American Society of Music Arrangers and Composers)
ASCAP (American Society of Composers, Authors, and Publishers)
BMI (Broadcast Music, Inc.)

CMA (Country Music Association)
DiMA (Digital Media Association)
GMA (Gospel Music Association)
GMS (Guild of Music Supervisors)
HFA (Harry Fox Agency)
ISME (International Society for Music Education)
ISPA (International Society for the Performing Arts)
LAO (League of American Orchestras)
MIDEM (Marché International du Disque et de l'Édition Musicale)
Music Business Association – Music Biz
NAfME (National Association for Music Education)
NAMM (National Association of Music Merchants)
NARIP (National Association of Recording Industry Professionals)
NMPA (National Music Publishers Association)
NSAI (Nashville Songwriters Association International)
RIAA (Recording Industry Association of America)
SAG-AFTRA (Screen Actors Guild - American Federation of Television and Radio Artists)
SCL (Society of Composers & Lyricists)
SESAC (Society of European Stage Authors and Composers)
SGA (Songwriter Guild of America)
SoundExchange
SPARS (Society of Professional Audio Recording Studios)
The Recording Academy (a/k/a National Academy of Recording Arts & Sciences)
WFMT (World Federation of Music Therapy)
WMBA (Women's Music Business Association)

The Business Of Music

Wherever your music interest takes you, you are in the business of music.

When starting out, most musicians lack the business skills to plan for the future. Taking care of the business side of music can be overwhelming, but that's only when you're not clear on what you should be doing and how to do it properly. Regardless of what field of music you are interested in, there are unique business components related to it.

Serious players in music understand the music business. Obviously, no one knows everything, but pretending that music is not a business, and not taking the time to learn all you can about it, is asking for trouble.

Trusting your instincts that tell you when to rely on the knowledge of others is another skill set worth developing; so never be afraid to ask questions.

Some of the following topics will apply more to some careers than others, but there are books, classes and online courses that cover all of these in much greater detail.

This is just a starter list to help you become aware of areas of which you may not be familiar with:

> Administration agreements
> Royalty advances
> American Federation of Musicians membership/agreements
> Artist/producer royalty clauses
> Composing, songwriting, arranging, and conducting agreements
> Compulsory licenses
> Controlled composition clauses
> Copyright law - domestic and international
> Copyright registration/ownership/sale/acquisition
> Distribution agreements
> Lawyers, managers, agents – roles and agreements
> Master use licensing agreements
> Mechanical licenses
> Music cue sheets
> Performance rights organizations (ASCAP/BMI/SESAC, etc.)
> Publishing/Co-publishing/Sub-publishing agreements
> Record/360 contracts
> Synchronization licenses
> Works made for hire

Show Me The Money!

Even though the international music business is worth approximately $26 billion US per year, it's probably not a great career choice if you're going into music to make boatloads of money. People have very different financial goals; but the focus should be to be able to love what you are doing while you are doing what you love.

Let's first address the elephant in the room. The answer to "Can I make a living in music?" is a frustrating yes... and no, although everyone has a definition of what they feel is necessary to consider their income a "living." As you would expect, there is a huge swing in income possibilities given the wide range of career options.

There are certain areas in music where income is more strictly defined, such as education, where a music teacher's salary is determined by the community, institution and geographic region. Of course, there are career tracks accompanied by significant sums of money *if* the right combination of events and talent intersect.

Still, a passion for your chosen field should be your driving force.

If you're just starting out, making money probably falls into one of these categories:
You can:
> arrange, produce, create beats or perform on other people's music
> record and stream music or post your music on sites like Bandcamp
> sell merchandise (music, lyrics, apparel, etc. - live and online)
> play/DJ live locally as a solo artist or with a group
> give private music lessons
> play events, parties, bars, etc.
> license your recordings or songs for others to use

But be sure to refer to the "Music Gigs-A-Plenty" chapter to get your creativity flowing about other areas where your talent can shine *and* be monetized.

Show Me More Money!!

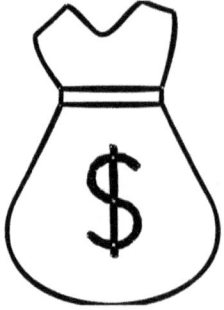 

Fear of financial instability is a very legitimate concern when considering a music career. Understanding the sources of income and how the music business works can help alleviate some of the anxiety. I'll give you a little taste of it, but the more you hunger to have a deeper knowledge of what income streams are available to you, the more prepared – and confident – you can be.

While traditional music professions (like teaching) may reduce long-term concerns, because of their perceived stability, diversifying income streams to help sustain you during slower times of your career is a smart move - especially with a self-employed livelihood.

And here is a *golden nugget*. Every area of the music ecosystem mentioned in the chapter Music Gigs-A-Plenty can create income; but with some professions, you can enjoy additional income, in the form of royalties, residuals or commissions, for many years after the original music was created.

Passive income, back-end money, or what some affectionately call "mailbox money", is income that generates itself because you have ownership or have contributed in some way that allows you to share in the monetization of musical works. Some back-end money is based on a negotiation at the beginning of a project, and some are defined by legislation or governing entities over which you have no control.

Just A Taste of Copyrights and Publishing

Understanding what is meant by copyright ownership and publishing rights are important topics for every musician. It can also be very confusing, and there are volumes of books written on the subject, but here is a very short introduction to help get you started:

The main law in the United States that governs musical compositions and all other intellectual property is called the U.S. Copyright Act. If you write an original song (for this example, but all musical works apply), the Copyright Act says that you own all rights in that song from the moment of creation. You actually don't have to do anything to confirm that, but if you want to make sure that the rest of the world knows you wrote something, it is best to put it into a tangible form such as a recording or a printing of your lyrics and music. And while you do not have to register a song with the US Copyright Office, it is recommended that you do so because you preserve certain additional legal rights that become important if there is a dispute about the song.

The Copyright Act also gives each author additional exclusive rights to control each creation - but only for a finite period. The *term of copyright* for works written after 1978 is defined as the "life of the author plus 70 years." And if you co-write the song with other people, the Copyright Act says that everyone owns the song in equal shares unless you designate a different split in writing.

In terms of revenue that flows from the use of a song, the music world recognizes that, generally speaking, each dollar earned is divided in half: 50% is deemed to be the "writer's share" (split among all co-writers) and 50% is deemed to be the "publisher's share".

As the owner of the copyright, you have the right to:
1) decide how, and when, you want to make it first available to the public;
2) decide how your song (or recording) is used;
3) choose how you want to make money with your work;
4) sell or license your work;
5) engage a publisher or publishing company.
(The publisher is the person or entity that you have designated to administer or manage the activities of the song. If you do it yourself, then you are considered your own publisher.)

It's all one big pie that comes down to individual slices - so let's eat!

Money That Comes From Songs & Compositions

#1-Public Performance Income
Enjoying what is called "performance income" requires membership in a performing rights organization such as ASCAP, BMI, SESAC or SoundExchange (for digital performances), which act as collecting agents and distribute royalties to songwriters, composers and publishers. Examples of where your music might be heard that generates royalties are terrestrial radio, satellite radio, streaming services, TV, movies, webcasters, as well as live performances at theatres, concert venues, bars, clubs, etc.

#2-Mechanical Royalty
The term "mechanical" goes back to the copyright law of 1909 when Congress established a royalty that needed to be paid when a musical composition was "mechanically" played on a player piano. The term is still used today but broadly refers to the reproduction of your music via any physical or digital methods.

You are entitled to a mechanical royalty on every copy or unit sold or licensed that contains your song. Thus, the sale of physical reproductions such as vinyl and CDs generate mechanical royalties that are payable to you by the entity that distributed the recording (e.g., a record label or indie distributor). Mechanical royalties are also triggered (and payable by your digital service provider) each time a recorded song is streamed or downloaded.

Under the Copyright Act, you decide who can record your song first. But there is a special provision that says that, once a song is first publicly available, anyone else can also record it without your permission as long as they pay you (or your publisher) the current mechanical royalty for each copy sold.

The rate for a mechanical royalty is established by the Copyright Royalty Board, which is a part of the U.S. Copyright Act, and is subject to increase over time.

The Harry Fox Agency is one of the largest and oldest companies, but not the only one, whose business is to issue mechanical licenses and to collect and distribute royalties on behalf of music creators and owners.

#3-Print publishing Royalty
Sheet music is a revenue stream that is often overlooked.

If you write a song or composition that lends itself to being played or adapted in other musical forms, print and online publishers such as Hal Leonard and Alfred Music have extensive catalogs in the area of sheet music for band, orchestra, choral, piano, symphonic, studies for individual instruments, and many more categories.

Whether physical, digital, individual sheet music, or as part of a folio, royalties are paid on every sale or download.

#4-Licensing your music
(see 8a below)

Money That Comes From Making Records

#5-Producer Royalty
If you are a Producer, you may commonly receive compensation from an up-front fee. Still, the key will be to negotiate "points," which is a percentage of revenue created by the work and defines what monies you'll be entitled to in the future.

#6-Artist Royalty
A key part of a record deal with a record label will be your artist royalty rate, which is paid as a percentage of sales. This topic has many nuances and is beyond the scope of this book to go deeper. However, suppose you are not signed to a record label and, instead, distribute your music as an independent artist. In that case, your royalties are automatically included in payments made to you by the digital service provider (DSP) or distributor.

#7-Streaming Royalty
Monetizing your music that is used on social media platforms including Facebook, Instagram, Tik Tok, Apple Music, Spotify, and other digital platforms, generally requires distribution from companies (as of this writing) such as TuneCore, CD Baby, or DistroKid, which also help ensure that accurate metadata is attached. Terms can vary greatly, and even though streaming generally pays fractions of a penny per stream, those pennies can still add up over time.

#8-Licensing Fees
License your music.

If you're ready to put your music out there, there's a good chance there are places for it to be heard, since anywhere you hear music is a place that could presumably be using yours!

A benefit to licensing is that you are able to grant permission for your work to be used while you retain all the ownership rights. In some cases, you can negotiate the terms and options for its specific use, but often it can simply be a take-it or leave-it offer.

The fees for this type of use can vary from $0 to large sums of money, depending on how in demand your music is. Even if the up-front money may seem low, it can be shortsighted to not license it, especially if the use may have longevity. The important thing to remember is that whenever this music is used, it generates performance income. And, depending on the number and type of uses, it can lead to sustained income – sometimes many years after it was first licensed.

There are always two parts to this type of licensing:
> A): The licensing of the publishing rights (the composition itself) occurs through a synchronization license – often just called "the synch". This allows the song to be synchronized with an audio/visual product such as a television show, movie, video game, website, etc. The fee for this license is split between the songwriter and publisher, as are the royalties its use generates.

> B): The other license is a *master use license* – often just called "the master" - and grants the rights to the use of the recording itself, whether it exists in a digital, vinyl, CD, or a format not yet known.

If you wrote, published, and recorded your own song, your combined fee for the synch and master goes to you. But there can often be co-writers, co-publishers, companies or administrators that have approval rights and share the revenue.

- Additional Revenue Sources –

#9-Commissions
Music-related careers such as an artist agent, booking agent or manager are paid by a combination of salaries and/or commissions derived from money paid under the deal or agreement negotiated by the agent. The percentage usually has an expectation of being in alignment with the current industry standards but can also be negotiable.

#10-Union Residuals

Many professional musicians join the union known as the American Federation of Musicians (AFM). Union recording sessions are recorded under the rules set forth by the AFM, and provide the guidelines for fees and working conditions such as the length of sessions and required "breaks". If you perform on a soundtrack, TV, album or motion picture score under a union agreement, it can generate additional monies through the life of the recordings through re-use and new-use payments, special payments and the Film Musicians Secondary Market Fund.

For vocalists, the union governing those recordings and residuals is the Screen Actors Guild – American Federation of Television and Radio Artists (SAG-AFTRA).

Why The Heck Not

place your bucket list here

Have you ever thought to yourself, I'd love to speak to, or watch someone, doing something I might want to consider as a career?

Once, when I was on the road, the advance promotional team offered a unique experience to cast members, *if* they had free time in between performances. The question to the cast member was, "What would you like to do for an afternoon *if* you could do anything?"

The answers ranged from police ride-a-longs to observing chefs in a restaurant kitchen. Mine was to observe air traffic controllers do what they do. Along with music, I've always been fascinated with flight, so it wasn't much of a stretch for me to ask for that opportunity.

My point is that students – *especially* - don't often realize that they are at an ideal point in their lives to reach out to people who may be less willing to help them down the road, when they may be professional peers. You are not competition *now*, AND you are not looking for a job. You are just looking for some education into an emerging interest of yours; an interest that the person you're reaching out to possibly had at the same age as you.

Don't get me wrong; there are lots of jerks out there who could care less about giving time to a stranger that's trying to reach them.

But, what if that person admires the tenacity it took to find them, and is willing to go the extra mile to share lessons that might help you succeed? Don't underestimate the kindness of people to just let you observe and learn about a skill or craft you are interested in. Conversely, don't overestimate it either. Compassionate and very busy professionals who are laser-focused on their careers can often be unresponsive.

In my time as head of music for Paramount Pictures Television, I would occasionally get those calls. One call came from a student in the Midwest who was coming to Hollywood and wanted to watch the music for the television series *Star Trek: The Next Generation* being recorded (scored). After being transferred numerous times, the call found its way to me. I immediately embraced the resourcefulness of this young man and invited him and his parents to watch a recording session taking place on the studio lot with 65 of some of the best studio musicians in the world. He also got the opportunity to spend some time with the composer, ask questions about the process and take the studio tour for free!

If you don't take rejection personally, there's no reason not to try any crazy idea that might enter your mind. The worst that can happen is that you're back where you started. And the best part is that it never costs anything to ask.

You might even learn what may work more effectively on your next attempt!

> "You miss 100% of the shots you don't take."
> -Wayne Gretzky

To Music College – Or Not

Part 1

If you're reading this chapter, then you may be wondering if pursuing a music degree is for you. Asking if it's worth it or if it will really make a difference to your musical aspirations is a very valid question; but the answer is not as simple as you might like it to be. While it's not very satisfying to just say, "it depends," that's the appropriate response. However, let's dig a little deeper to try and look at the big picture.

Sorry to put it so bluntly, but don't be naïve. A music degree does not guarantee employment. But then again, no degree does. And even with other professions, what was once considered a "safe" degree may no longer hold the same confidence it once did. However, a degree in the arts has always held the dubious distinction of being perceived as risky.

I recall sharing my frustration with my mother about not being able to get consistent gigs when I first got to Los Angeles. She sounded perplexed and asked if I was letting people know I had a Berklee College of Music degree. She seemed to feel that the degree would open doors the way a law degree might be a calling card for a job at a law firm. It was then that I enlightened her that, as an instrumentalist, you either have the "chops" (a musician's term for ability) or you don't; how you acquired the skill is irrelevant to the listener. She wasn't very happy with that response.

Going to college may have been a one-size-fits-all in another century, but today's musician has more options than ever before, and a formal college education may - or may not be - precisely what's needed. The bottom line is that a music degree isn't for everyone and is a must-have for some. Some people know immediately that a structured environment isn't right for them, while others do not. It's OK not to know. And while gap years are a popular alternative, it can be daunting for some to change gears again after settling into a post-high school routine.

And the reality of some personal situations may lead you to the only possible decision. For example: you may not be able to leave the area you live in; the entrance requirements may be overly challenging; you may only have an option for a 2-year program; finances are a hardship; or you are scholarship- dependent.

Part 2

There are traditional and non-traditional ways to get an education, and since you are the collective of all you experience in life, every day presents opportunities to learn, regardless of whether you're on a campus. *My* choice was to embrace a 4-year curriculum where I knew what to expect as a requirement for graduation. I also wanted a degree for self-satisfaction which, as a footnote, was a pre-requisite 20 years later when I decided to pursue a higher education degree. However, music college may not be suitable for you if you know your out-of-college experiences will prepare you for exactly what you want to do. I've known musicians who have been very happy with their decision to study privately and have gone on to have significant careers. Others received their desired education from in-person summer programs or shorter-term music programs.

And then there is the hybrid choice: when I went to Berklee, some musicians would come in for a semester or two, only take the courses that interested them and then leave to go on tour, try the studio scene, teach privately, etc.

Today, many colleges offer that same approach via their online studies.

Not obtaining a music degree can create a challenging obstacle if you want to be a candidate for specific jobs. Some career choices make the question about a music degree very easy to answer. For example, you will need a music degree if you want to be a music educator at any accredited institution.

If you are college-bound, a structured environment will most likely nurture and develop your music aspirations. It's also a time for safe exploration, as you get exposed to unfamiliar fields, and to identify where your interests and talent soar. Conversely, it can also be a time to learn what (and who) doesn't sync with you personally and professionally.

The benefit also extends to meeting like-minded, motivated people who can become life-long friends, business associates, partners and collaborators. And great instructors can also become mentors and invaluable resources to guide you in your journey.

A degree also immediately validates you as having an intimate understanding of theory, harmony and music in general. It's a credential you'll carry for a lifetime, and you can choose when and where you want to share the accomplishment.

Whatever your situation, keep your eye on the ball, stay focused on the big picture, and remember that music is a *long game*.

What Should My Music Major Be?

Is your quest to become a famous performer? do you like producing beats? or maybe you want to teach in the public school system? The answer to those types of questions is the first step in determining which degree track you should consider.

Doesn't it make sense to study something that echoes your strengths as you consider a career in which you plan to be happy and successful? A performance degree is an obvious choice for an instrumentalist, or if you are fascinated with music history and the evolution of musical form, style, and instruments, then a degree in musicology may be your calling. Do you imagine yourself working in the music management field or the legal arena of musical copyrights?

Try to make a correlation between what gets you excited, what seems to come to you naturally, and what fields check *most* of your boxes… at least today. And don't forget to check the Music Gigs-A-Plenty chapter!

If you're unsure, try not to get too hung up on what career track you choose as it's very common to start with one interest, only to be introduced later on to another area that you find more interesting.

It's also likely that the first-year curriculum may be very similar at many music schools, colleges, universities and conservatories, and include core classes in ear training, harmony, theory, music history, composition and studies on your principal instrument. And if you are in a degree program, there will also be general (non-music) education classes that will be required - which may not be required in a certificate or similar program.

The levels of music degrees are the same as in most other fields, starting with an associate degree. After that, it's a bachelors, a masters, and then a doctorate, with each degree building on the studies that came before. Obtaining higher degrees might be based on desired personal and professional growth or dictated by a specific career goal that necessitates additional graduate studies.

As you'll quickly discover, the variety of courses is very broad. For example, Berklee's Independent Recording & Production degree teaches students how to produce professional quality music anywhere with a computer and DAW (digital audio workstation). It also offers a scoring degree for video games and interactive media.

Which College

Every year approximately 27,000 music degrees are awarded in the United States on top of anyone's guess of how many non-college-bound people commit annually to going into a music career domestically and around the world. So how do you choose what college will be the right place to give you the tools you'll need to be successful _and_ differentiate yourself from others?

Well, that's an excellent question!

You may start by asking yourself, "What [musician, producer, educator, performer, etc.] do I admire? Where did they study? What institutions do they support or mention in interviews?

You may not know exactly what you want from a college, but you probably have more of an idea than you may think.

Do you have an opinion on any of the following questions:

1) What is my preferred campus size? Do I thrive as a big fish in a small pond or a small fish in a big pond?
2) Geographic location? Do I want to take this opportunity to live in a different climate? How important is the local music scene to me?
3) Do I want a degree I can tailor with a flexible curriculum?
4) Do I want a faith-based institution?
5) What is the average class size? (which affects the effort it takes to make relationships with the professors)
6) What are housing options on and off campus? How long do people usually live on campus?
7) What is the institution's reputation?
8) Am I interested in clubs, sports, campus organizations, fraternity/sororities, recreational facilities, etc.?
9) Is a renowned faculty critical?
10) Is a diverse student body important to me?
11) What is the alumni network like?
12) Is the school involved in community/philanthropic work that interests me?
13) Do I want a student body that has other creative majors so that I'm interacting with multiple disciplines of the arts?

Thoroughly explore websites, do an in-person visit if possible, and reach out to others who have attended the college to find out what they thought of their experiences with the institution you may be considering.

Lots Of Music Colleges And Schools

I'm sure you have heard of many of the schools listed below, but there may be some that are new to you:

Baldwin Wallace Conservatory of Music (Berea, OH)
Bard College Conservatory of Music (Annandale-on-Hudson, NY)
Belmont University (Nashville, TN)
Berklee College of Music (Boston, MA)
Biola University Conservatory of Music (La Mirada, CA)
Birmingham–Southern Conservatory of Music (Birmingham, AL)
Bob Cole Conservatory of Music - California State University (Long Beach, CA)
Boston Conservatory at Berklee (Boston, MA)
Boston University School of Music (Boston, MA)
Brigham Young University - School of Music (Provo, UT)
Brooklyn College - Conservatory of Music (New York, NY)
Cadek Conservatory - University of Tennessee (Knoxville, TN)
Capital University Conservatory of Music (Bexley, OH)
Carnegie Mellon School of Music - Carnegie Mellon University (Pittsburgh, PA)
Chapman University Conservatory of Music (Orange, CA)
Chicago College of Performing Arts - Roosevelt University (Chicago, IL)
Cleveland Institute of Music (Cleveland, OH)
Columbia College Chicago (Chicago, IL)
Concordia College Conservatory (Bronxville, NY)
Cornish College of the Arts (Seattle, WA)
Curtis Institute of Music (Philadelphia, PA)
Drexel University (Philadelphia, PA)
Duquesne University - Mary Pappert School of Music (Pittsburgh, PA)
Eastman School of Music - University of Rochester (Rochester, NY)
Florida State University College of Music (Tallahassee, FL)
Frost School of Music - University of Miami (Coral Gables, FL)
Interlochen Arts Academy (Interlochen, MI)
Ithaca College School of Music (Ithaca, NY)
Jacobs School of Music - Indiana University (Bloomington, IN)
Kean University - Music Conservatory (Union, NJ)

La Jolla Conservatory of Music (La Jolla, CA)
Lawrence University Conservatory of Music (Appleton, WI)
Lionel Hampton School of Music - University of Moscow (Moscow, ID)
Los Angeles College of Music (Pasadena, CA)
LSU School of Music (Baton Rouge, LA)
Lynn University Conservatory of Music (Boca Raton, FL)
Manhattan School of Music (New York, NY)
Mannes School of Music - The New School (New York, NY)
Moores School of Music - University of Houston (Houston, TX)
Musicians Institute (Los Angeles, CA)
New England Conservatory (Boston, MA)
Northwestern University - Bienen School of Music (Evanston, IL)
NYU Steinhardt (New York, NY)
Oberlin Conservatory of Music - Oberlin College (Oberlin, OH)
Peabody Institute - Johns Hopkins University (Baltimore, MD)
Roosevelt University - Conservatory of Music (Chicago, IL)
Saint Mary-of-the-Woods Conservatory of Music (Saint Mary-of-the-Woods, IN)
San Francisco Conservatory of Music (San Francisco, CA)
Sarah and Ernest Butler School of Music - The University of Texas at Austin (Austin, TX)
Shenandoah University Conservatory (Winchester, VA)
Shepherd School of Music - Rice University (Houston, TX)
State University of New York at Fredonia - Fredonia School of Music (Fredonia, NY)
State University of New York at Potsdam - Crane School of Music, (Potsdam, NY)
State University of New York at Purchase - Conservatory of Music (Purchase, NY)
Sunderman Conservatory of Music - Gettysburg College (Gettysburg, PA)
Syracuse University - Setnor School of Music (Syracuse, NY)
The Colburn School (Los Angeles, CA)
The Hartt School - University of Hartford (West Hartford, CT)
The Juilliard School (New York, NY)
The New School for Jazz and Contemporary Music (New York, NY)
The University of the Arts (Philadelphia, PA)
UCLA Herb Alpert School of Music (Los Angeles, CA)

UNCG School of Music, Theatre and Dance (Greensboro, NC)
University of Cincinnati College - Conservatory of Music (Cincinnati, OH)
University of Colorado - Boulder College of Music (Boulder, CA)
University of Mary Hardin–Baylor - Conservatory of Music (Belton, TX)
University of Maryland - School of Music (College Park, MD)
University of Miami - Frost School of Music (Miami, FL)
University of Michigan School of Music, Theatre & Dance (Ann Arbor, MI)
University of Missouri - Kansas City Conservatory (Kansas City, MO)
University of Missouri School of Music (Columbia, MO)
University of North Carolina School of the Arts (Winston-Salem, NC)
University of North Texas College of Music (Denton, TX)
University of Oregon School of Music and Dance (Eugene, OR)
University of the Pacific - Conservatory of Music (Stockton, CA)
USC Thornton School of Music (Los Angeles, CA)
Vanderbilt University - Blair School of Music (Nashville, TN)
VanderCook College of Music (Chicago, IL)
Westminster Choir College - Rider University (Lawrenceville, NJ)
Wheaton College - Conservatory of Music (Wheaton, IL)
Wilkes University Conservatory of Music (Wilkes-Barre, PA)
Yale School of Music - Yale University (New Haven, CT)

The World Of Musical Styles

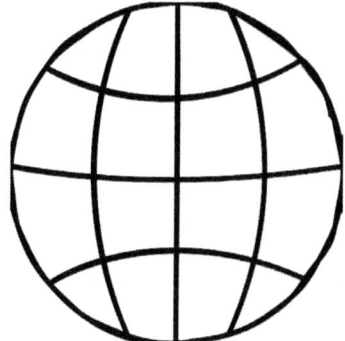

Have you ever heard of Motswako or Grime music? If you haven't, you are probably not alone. Each one of the styles below started as a moment of inspiration by its creator(s) and developed into a style that represents the culture and personality of the environment surrounding it. After that, it expanded into the music ecosystem to be enjoyed or adapted by the creative juices of new listeners.

There's a good chance you won't relate to many of the styles but try to listen to what makes it - *it*. What are the notes used in the scale? What are the instruments being played? What dynamics and articulations are being played? What time signatures are used, and are they combined in ways that are foreign to you? How is the arrangement like or unlike what you are familiar with? What recording or production techniques are being employed?

If you hear generic music in the elevator, most people probably dismiss it. What happens when you listen to it analytically? What's the style? For example, what if you were listening to a bossa nova, which uses a traditional rhythmic pattern commonly played with clave sticks? Could a bossa nova rhythm be something that might influence what you are working on now, later or next year? What did you like or dislike about it? What would you have done differently if you had been the writer, arranger, performer or producer? Emerge from that elevator with another sound or feel to put in your musical toolbox.

When you consider overlaying your choices with the fraction of styles listed below, the combinations yet to be created are infinite – and unique.

The list on the following pages is just a small sampling of styles from around the world.

Expand your mind and your music awareness by exploring them with open ears and an open mind:

Acid house
Acid jazz
Acid rock
Acousmatic
Alternative R&B
Alternative rock
Ambient dub
Baithak Gana
Ballroom dance
Baltimore club
Baroque
Baroque pop
Bluegrass
Bongo flava
Broadway
Cajun
Calypso
Cantopop
Cha-cha-chá
Chicago hard house
Chicago blues
Children's
Chillwave
Christian rock

Classical
Cloud rap
Country blues
Country rock
Crunk
Dancehall pop
Dark ambien
Delta blues
Detroit blues
Disco polo
Doo-wop
Doomcore
Drill
Dubstyle
Electro-disco
Electro-industrial
Electronicore
Elevator
Ethnic electronica
Eurodance
Europop
Fann at-Tanbura
Film and television
Folk

Folktronica
Funk rock
Funkstep
Future house
Gamelan
Garage punk
Garage rock
Ghettotech
Gospel
Gothic metal
Gregorian chant
Hardcore punk
Hip hop soul
Hip house
Hokum blues
Honky-tonk
House music
Hypnagogic pop
Jazz rock
K-pop
Kawaii future bass
Kawaii metal
Liquid funk
Louisiana swamp pop
Mambo
Marches
Medieval
Memphis blues
Merengue
Military
Mumble rap
National anthems
Neo soul
Neo-progressive rock
New Mexico
New wave
New Jack Swing
Nu skool breaks

Piedmont blues
Pop sunda
Polka
Progressive rock
Psychedelic rock
Punta rock
Ragga jungle
Red dirt
Reggae
Renaissance
Rock and roll
Rumba
Sakara
Salsa
Sea shantie
Shamstep
Ska
Skate punk
Sludge metal
Soul
Southern rock
Street punk
Sunshine pop
Synth-pop
Techno
Tango
Tejano
Thai pop
Timba
Tribal house
Turkish pop
Urban Pasifia
Videogame
Viking metal
Worldbeat
Yodeling
Zouk
Zydeco

The Superstars Speak

Question: What would you tell your 17 to 22 year-old self on how to have a long-term successful career in any facet of music?

This question was given to 19 extremely successful professionals ages 25 through 80. I have kept their names anonymous so that any bias does not diminish the impact of their wisdom. Still, whatever your age or stage of your career, their answers are timeless and universally applicable.

Their fields of success are listed below, and they have collectively been awarded Grammys, Oscars, Emmys, gold records and accolades from dozens of other significant organizations. It's not an overstatement to say that the impact of their contributions has generated billions of dollars, and has been appreciated by more people on the planet than can be possibly estimated.

> Motion Picture Composer
> Motion Picture Director
> Motion Picture Producer
> Music Agent
> Music Attorney

- Music College professor/department chair
- Music Editor
- Music Journalist
- Music orchestrator/arranger
- Music store owner
- Music Supervisor
- Production Music Composer
- Record Producer
- Record/stage/studio singer
- Sideman Musician
- Solo Musician/artist
- Songwriter
- Television Composer
- Television Producer

The folks that do these jobs had to have learned something valuable and here it is!:

Great advice from very successful music people

"Don't be afraid to make mistakes or ask for help."

"Create a niche with your uniqueness, since no one is better at being you than you."

"Whatever music career you focus on is a smaller community than you think and everything you do and say *now*, creates your reputation."

"Don't let rejection, or what other people say you can't do, keep you from moving forward. Be who you are and care less about what others think."

"Never turn down any opportunity to have any musical experience."

"Music is a social business. Learn to be comfortable introducing yourself to strangers and engaging others in conversation."

"Talent + preparation will prepare you for the opportunities that await you."

"If you get a "no," it is only "no" at the moment. Things change. Be persistent but be polite because you never know when the timing might be perfect."

"Openness, flexibility, and resiliency will take you to unpredicted and unexpected places. Be ready to say yes."

"Don't miss opportunities by dwelling on past mistakes."

"When you get along with others, they'll want to work with you and recommend you. Be kind: No one wants to work with a jerk."

"If it's in your soul and you love what you do, then commit to going all the way, but not because you're chasing money. And then push further."

"Meaningful relationships are 90% of what the music business is all about. Stay in touch with people you meet over the years."

"Be prepared to do everything necessary to over-deliver and be the absolute best at what you say you'll do. People quickly learn who they can count on and you never know who's paying attention to your efforts."

"The way you see something is the way only you can see it. Remember that you have a unique perspective to share with the world."

"Ingredients for long-term success include your ability to communicate, collaborate, actively listen, think creatively, and to be empathetic."

"Network where people are doing what it is you want to do, since there's nothing like face-to-face interactions."

"Find other like-minded people to be friends with; take them seriously and learn from them."

"Have thick skin, objectivity and get educated, regardless of your music career choice."

"It's not enough to just love music or hope for a career. You need to know your chosen field inside and out, where it's headed and with knowledge about the music business.

Math/Schmath!

You may love math – which is excellent. But then again, like me, you may not - which is why it's ironic that I ended up getting a master's degree in business which requires a lot of math. That's not a common educational path for a musician, but I realized later in life that it's very helpful to have a good understanding of "usable" math - no matter what you do. Whether you become an employee or are self-employed, understanding finances and establishing good money habits will have lifetime benefits. Conversely, making choices that can hinder your goals personally and professionally doesn't take very long. Fortunately, many apps and programs can help you track your money, regardless of your income.

If you think of yourself at any age or situation as running a small business, it can help frame your thinking. It doesn't matter how old you are or how much money is in the equation. Learning healthy ways to track and spend lays the groundwork for good credit scores, translating into *many* financial opportunities, including the ability to borrow money when needed and *especially* for buying the tools for your career choice.

Where you are in your career will have a significant bearing on how you budget your money. As an example, living in a dormitory does not require you to budget for house payments, but you have other expenses now that you won't have down the line. How you allocate your money will change over time, but many constants remain.

It doesn't need to be a daunting task; to the contrary, it may free up some energy to focus on other things, if your mind knows you're doing the best you can with the money you've got.

Income is income, and it doesn't matter if it comes from an allowance, gift, a gig or a paycheck. It can still be broken into separate categories to help get you the most "bang for your buck."

Think of it as "buckets". The names of your "buckets" may change, but for now let's focus on four:

Saving and Charity

Two of the buckets are very simple. The first is to **SAVE**. I'm sure you've heard it before, but regardless of how you choose to save, you'll never be sorry you did. It does take some discipline, but once you start practicing it – like anything else – becomes much more manageable.

Opening a savings account that earns interest is a logical choice. There are also investment accounts that, with some guidance, can create a great opportunity to have your money work harder for you and be there when you need it most. While 10% of your income is a recommended amount to save, I suggest deciding on the most you feel you can *consistently* save, and then reevaluating the amount as time goes on.

The second bucket is **CHARITY**. For many people, the act of giving makes them feel gratitude and happiness and is especially rewarding when you're giving to something that you relate to. No matter what you care about - music, the environment, homelessness, etc. - there is an organization dedicated to improving the lives of the people involved. Any donated amount is always appreciated, even $1, and you'll probably never know the positive difference it might be making. Don't overthink it either, since donating can be as simple as contributing to a local fundraiser or dropping a few coins in a box supporting a national charity.

The act of giving is what's important and not the amount.

> "The difference between who you are and who you want to be is what you do."
> -Bill Phillips

Expenses/Fun Money

The next bucket is the biggest variable over time, which is your **EXPENSES**. As your obligations for things like gas, food or housing increase, you will need to track them more closely, especially if you're using debit or credit cards. Putting these *fixed costs* (meaning expenses that you will have no matter what else is happening in your life) first, will help you prioritize where your money should go. And don't be fooled by the attraction of just paying the minimum amount due. That's a fast-track to bigger financial problems because you will never pay off the balance.

The last bucket is your **FUN MONEY** for all the other stuff: gifts, entertainment, concerts, restaurants and, of course, the never-ending appetite of musicians for gear. Technically, these are called discretionary or non-restricted funds, and it's the most challenging category to keep under control.

Consider the difference between needing and wanting something. It's important to realize that the immediate gratification of getting something you *want* now may impact your ability to acquire something you'll *need* in the future. Thinking about it that way can help guide you to decisions you'll be the happiest with in the long run.

Be A Body Builder

This book is not about the obvious benefits of eating well and exercising. But let's face facts: it's common sense that if you mistreat your body on any level, your music and your music career goals will not be "firing on all cylinders." Education on this topic is as important as any other topic in your music career journey, but we all know intellectually that exercise and good food aid in good mental health, sound sleep, and an overall better lifestyle. Conversely, abusing drugs and alcohol dissociates you from your feelings and can, frankly, just stop good things from happening in your life.

I can summarize this subject by saying that it's never too early to be aware of what can negatively impact your ability to be all you want to be. Since that wouldn't make for much of a chapter, let's start by spending a few words on one of your most valued and irreplaceable senses for this career: your hearing!

I Hear You!

Would you drive in a car without a seatbelt? I'm guessing the answer is "no" for most people. But knowing the possible result of an accident by not wearing it motivates you to make the safe choice.

Your hearing is no different. But most people and musicians don't think about their hearing until they start to experience problems, and by that time they may have permanent damage to their inner ear. It's not loud music that is the concern; it's loud *sound* - no matter what's making it - plus its level, frequency and duration.

Guess what? The effect of loud sounds on your hearing accumulates over the years, so what starts as losing a bit of the higher frequencies expands over time. It can creep up on you without you realizing it since, at first, your ears can recover after harmful sound exposure. That's why even though your ears may be ringing after attending a loud concert, it eventually subsides.

Of course, you can't always avoid loud sounds when you're in the middle of playing with a group or at a concert that's louder than you thought it would be. As a rule of thumb, your ears can safely handle up to 85dba (decibels) for as long as 8 hours. That's the equivalent of a noisy restaurant, and what some consider the threshold for potential hearing damage. A low-end rock concert is 100dba, and your ears can handle it safely for only 15 minutes. At 115dba it's down to 30 seconds.

There's a reason organizations like HEAR (Hearing Education and Awareness for Rockers) stress the importance of safe hearing, and why Apple iPhones have audio level controls in the health app. It's also easier than ever to know how loud your environment is by downloading a free sound meter from an app store.

Years ago, musicians complained that earplugs decreased frequencies leaving speech and music muffled, but new technology has changed that. A quick internet search will lead you to the myriad of available cost-effective ear protection.

The thing to know is that hearing loss is often preventable. However, everyone's susceptibility to noise injury is somewhat different, and once loud sounds take it away... it's often irreversible.

OUCH!

As a drummer, I started moving my gear in and out of cars at a very early age. By high school, it was almost a daily event, and by college, and many years after, it *was* an everyday event. However, not until I started getting back pain did anyone educate me on the correct way to lift. The problem creeps up on you, but once I started having back issues, I learned I could have avoided the pain by making small changes earlier.

Your particular situation may not relate to moving drums. Still, various ailments can befall instrumentalists and vocalists over time, depending on what parts of your body are getting repetitive use. You probably won't be thinking much about it in the earlier years of your career, but doing some proactive research into simple ways to avoid long-term physical difficulties seems like a smart idea.

Treat Your Mind Like A Friend

Fortunately, our society has become more enlightened about the holistic nature of the human body and that mental and physical health unite for a happier existence. Being in the music business – in any form – can trigger lots of emotional highs and lows for some people, and can take its toll on mental well-being and life satisfaction. For example, as a performing musician, constant exposure to being critiqued by peers and the public, plus erratic income, can be a continuous source of concern, stress and anxiety that may erode one's confidence level.

Too many people in the music industry have lost their lives to mental illness, drugs and alcohol.

One study suggests that 73 percent of musicians experience depression or anxiety. That is an unsettling percentage, and it seems to be specifically referring to freelance instrumentalists, but there are unique factors at play here, such as long hours of practicing alone and the inconsistency of work.

When referring to any freelance music career choice where you don't have the structure of a company or corporation, you are your boss and the destiny of your future. Of course, there are pros and cons to this, but how you navigate the challenges ultimately depends on your tolerance level for the ups and downs of the industry. And while it's easy to focus on negative experiences versus positive ones, when the good stuff happens, try writing it down to remind you later how good it felt.

> "The right place values you the right way. If you are not valued, don't be angry, it just means you're in the wrong place. Never stay in a place where no one sees your value."
> -Anonymous

Many people credit the practice of meditation or yoga as sources of relaxation, creativity and focus. There are so many apps, websites, and in-person opportunities to try these for free and while it may not be for everyone, the barrier to trying it out is very low.

Another easy avenue is walking or hiking. Finding a few moments in nature to create a different setting can sometimes be a simple way to create a positive frame of mind.

Asking for help has never been easier. At the time of this writing, organizations such as MusicCares, Backline, Music Industry Therapist Collective, and Sweet Relief Musicians Fund are there to help. There will always be a need for these types of organizations, and while the names may change - the mission won't – so just search a bit more generally and you'll find support.

Stories From the Real World

The following stories are for your entertainment. They are real-life situations I encountered, including a few life lessons learned from actual musical experiences. I hope you enjoy them.

It's All About the Music

I was producing a CBS television theme song for a new series written by a world-famous lyricist team, an Emmy, Grammy, Oscar, and Tony award-winning songwriter/composer; and a singer who had sold more than 100 million records.

The songwriter had hired a guitarist as the lead instrument, but at the end of the day felt strongly that the guitar part should have been played on the piano. As tired as he was, he replaced the guitar recording with his piano playing, and we all went home. Although he was an exceptional pianist, the recording didn't feel quite right – probably because we spent the day fine-tuning the guitar performance but had little time to work on the piano. As time passed, the producers decided a new piano recording was needed to make it perfect. Unfortunately, the songwriter was not available for quite a while.

Since I play piano (as well as drums), I decided to record a temporary piano track until a new session could be scheduled and, after having heard the song so many times, was quite confident I could do it justice. As time went on, everyone became very comfortable with my recording and no longer felt a need to have a new one recorded. It was my job to make the call to let the songwriter know that his piano track would not be used.

This was not a phone call I looked forward to making.

The songwriter's response? "It's not about me. It's about what's right for the music. If your track is a better choice for the recording, then that's the track the song needs to have." I thought to myself, "What a classy and inspirational answer."

Don't Ignore Your Blind Spots

Under the heading of "Don't ignore your blind spots", here is a lesson I learned the hard way. There was a well-known singer I desperately wanted to play for, and I was fortunate enough to have crossed paths with her music director on multiple occasions. While in Los Angeles producing demos for this singer, he finally called me for a session. However, before I tell you about the session, it's important to know what caused this opportunity to become my worst nightmare.

I was a pretty good drummer at this point in my career, playing professionally and continuing to practice every day, but I had areas I needed to focus on, like any musician. One such area centered on locking into a nice continuous groove playing 1/16 notes with my right hand on my hi-hat at 98 beats-per-minute (bpm) or greater. I knew faster tempos would require alternating from my right to the left hand, but it would result in a noticeably different feel.

It's not like I worried much about this issue, as it was just one of those kinks that would work itself out over time. I could always groove with 1/8 notes at any tempo, which would be my backup approach, but 1/16 notes with one hand above 98 bpm was some serious kryptonite.

With a few minutes left before the session started, I sat at my drums and looked over the chart, which was very simple and bolstered my self-confidence for the upcoming recording. The chart specifically called for a smooth 1/16 note feel on the hi-hat, but within seconds I knew I was in trouble. The tempo was *exactly* 99 bpm, and they wanted to use an electronic metronome called a click-track so there would be no fluctuation in the tempo.

I instinctively tried the alternating sticking, which was the wrong feel entirely, and after the bass player shot me a look, I slipped into unacceptable 1/8 notes. While I hoped it wouldn't happen, the music director stopped the recording and asked me to please "read the ink" (meaning to read the music exactly) and apply the 1/16 note hi-hat pattern as indicated. The rest of the session just went downhill from there, and when it was over I packed up my gear with my tail between my legs.

As you might expect, I never got any future work from my friend, but I did spend the next few weeks working on that issue so that it would never happen again!

Titanic Redux

You may remember the scene in the Titanic when the musicians decide to continue playing together as the ship sinks and you're touched by their camaraderie and artistry.

I had a similar experience on the morning of September 11, 2001.

The beginning of the five hour "Star Trek: Voyager" recording session with 65 musicians was set for 9:00 AM (PST). By then, the attacks on the East Coast were already being broadcast around the globe. As some of the world's best musicians entered the huge scoring stage on the Paramount Pictures lot, the topic of conversation was solely about what was happening in real-time. In addition, there was justifiable uncertainty about whether these attacks would be nationwide, and whether other high-profile locations, such as a motion picture and television studio, might also be potential targets.

At 9:00 AM on the dot, every musician expected at that session was in their respective place. I asked the composer and producer if I could have a minute on the conductor's podium to address the musicians about the unfolding world event. The studio lot was going into lockdown, but beyond that there had not been any word about how the crisis would be handled. The enormous studio facility could easily have 2,000 people working at one time, and there had not yet been enough time to process what was happening.

The hush was immediate, as I was not the one they were expecting to see on the conductor's podium. I said to them, honestly, that I had no idea what the immediate future held, but what I did know was that: 1) the session was going to continue until told otherwise; 2) anyone who felt uneasy about being there could leave with no repercussions for future work; and 3) anyone who did leave would still be fully compensated for the day.

Not one person made a move, not even a gesture to suggest they were considering it. They were there to make music as a community of professionals and, in solidarity, did just that.

Where the Heck is the Piano Player?

It was the 2nd half of a double recording session. The morning three hour session was very successful, and everyone was returning from lunch for the beginning of the 2nd three hour session. Seventy-four of the 75 musicians were sitting in their respective chairs, but one of the three keyboardists was nowhere to be found. His six electronic keyboards and racks of synthesizer equipment were right where he had left them in the morning, but his chair was empty.

The composer/conductor paced on the podium until he looked into the recording booth and asked, comically, yet seriously, "Does anyone in there play the piano?".

I had mentioned to the engineer earlier that I played some piano and, to be helpful, he pushed the talkback button and responded with an energetic "Grossman does!" I was there to supervise the session, not to play on it, but given the situation's urgency, I left the booth to join the other musicians.

One of the other keyboardists was kind enough to find the right sounds on the missing musicians' equipment so that all I had to do was play the music. The part was more complicated than I felt comfortable playing as written, but there was no time to back out. I quickly decided which sections I knew I could play, and avoided anything that looked problematic.

It was a real adrenaline rush that seemed to satisfy the immediate need!

Does Anyone Know How to Drum?

Musician union recording sessions are a minimum of three hours with an option to keep the musicians - with pay, of course - for an additional one hour. After that, they are free to leave, although overtime pays so well that most musicians will happily keep playing if they can.

As I sat in the booth looking at the amount of music that still needed to be recorded for an upcoming episode of a television series Paramount was producing, it became painfully clear that even the extra hour wouldn't be enough time. Once we got to the end of that hour, the music contractor asked if any of the musicians had a scheduling conflict that would require any of them to leave.

There was just the rhythm section left in the studio, and no one had a problem staying except... the drummer. He apologized and explained that he had allowed for the hold hour, but not for anything further and needed to leave to be on time for his next session. He came into the booth with sticks in hand and said, "Does anyone want to play my drums to finish the session?"

For a nano-second, everyone thought we'd have to accept that we didn't get all the music recorded until I raised my hand and said I'd be happy to sit in for the remaining music cues (the industry name for one segment of music). No one knew I had a professional background in drumming when I accepted his offer, took the sticks, and went into the drum booth.

While the musicians had a skeptical look as I sat down, that quickly dissipated when we started the first cue. Unfortunately, a stick broke in half almost immediately, and he had only left me the one pair! While I successfully played out the remainder of the session with one stick, I did so with a very unexpected handicap.

Naps Can Be Dangerous

Logic tells us that the right balance between physical and mental health positively impacts everything we do. Part of that balance is as simple as getting the right amount of sleep. That differs to certain degrees in each person, but getting very little sleep, mixed with putting extreme demands on your body, can have less than favorable results on most people, as was the case for me.

I was the principal drummer for a show that had multiple performances in one day at a huge theater whose backstage was filled with small dressing rooms, which were not all being used.

I can't remember why I thought I could do this, but during a 20-minute intermission for one of the shows, I felt so exhausted that I thought I could grab a 10-minute nap in one of those dressing rooms to "recharge" myself for the second half.

Imagine my shock when I awoke to the music that opened the second half of the show being performed by one of the percussionists - because no one could find me. I was able to slither behind the stage sets and lighting to the drum platform and switch with him at the end of the opening song. However, I had a lot of explaining to do after the show was over. I was embarrassed and apologetic that I let myself and the show down, but I learned the hard way the need to recognize the potential consequences of my choices.

Play Like You Mean It!

Here's a story that changed my drumming forever, although I'm not very proud of how it presented itself. I was still a teenager when I was on the road, and although I was playing the music right, I wasn't playing very musically. What I mean by that is I wasn't paying much attention to dynamics, *really* listening to the other players, playing as tastefully as I could, or being consistent in my starting tempos.

We were in a rehearsal one day with a British producer hired to increase the show's overall quality when he seemed to be giving me more suggestions than I thought I deserved. He also referenced drummers he had worked with when commenting to me, which finally annoyed me. I reacted by saying to him very sarcastically that "I was sorry I didn't play like his British drummers."

He smiled and very calmly said to me, "At least my British drummers play like they mean it". Ouch… I mean, OUCH! I slithered back to my drum kit and forever - and I mean it literally - played with more measured self-confidence and increased sensitivity to the players around me and the music. I have interpreted his words differently over the years, but it's always in search of trying to be a better musician.

Bonus Topics (mainly) For Instrumentalists and Vocalists

When you hear a song in the distance, ask yourself what the bpm (beats-per-minute) is. It's simple to get there by counting how many beats you hear in ten seconds and multiplying by six (because ten seconds times six equals one minute).

If there's no music to hear at the moment, listen to your heart. No, really. Take your pulse. Use that same formula to identify your heart's BPM.

There once was a car commercial that highlighted all the rhythms that are simultaneously around us - like the windshield wiper and the clicking of the turn signal. It's called a polyrhythm, when multiple rhythms are played on top of each other, and you don't need to be in a band or a music class to experience it. Rhythms are all around us if we take a moment to listen for them, and even conversations can be polyrhythmic.

Try and hear the rhythms of the world around you and, if you've acquired notation skills, jot down what you're hearing as part of your ear training.

Do you ever get a song stuck in your head? Rather than being annoyed by it, figure out what clicked with you. Was it the melody?, the chords?, the instruments?, the rhythm?, the lyrics?, the production technique?, the mix? Did you like the key modulation? If you are a songwriter, is there something about the song you particularly liked and would want to use? Conversely, were there elements of the song that you disliked and would like to avoid when creating your own music? Consider listening with headphones to get a more intimate experience with which to evaluate it.

Here's something fun to do in boring moments: Tap your finger on the table and decide what kind of note value it is. Is it a quarter, half or whole note? What is the tempo? Its possibilities are endless until the next beat - or your finger - sounds. And even then, did you tap out two quarter notes or eighth notes? Get it? Until the next beat appears, the time in between beats is infinite. It only finds its place in the rhythmic universe when you decide what its value is.

You can also practice playing on – in front of – or behind – the beat. Think about each downbeat falling on the "12" on your watch, and the next 60 seconds - or any increment of time - being the elapsed time before the next beat falls. You can either play right on the 12 or a second before or after – often referred to as playing in front of – or behind the beat - with an increased distance getting closer to rushing or dragging the beat, respectively.

What makes a musician musical? It's a tricky question to answer, but most would agree that it starts with *really* listening to the other musicians around you as you play with them. Listening in a way that it becomes not about you, but about the collective music you are creating - and choosing to play what fits. It might be about the dynamics or phrasing you use, how active you're playing, or whether you <u>should</u> be playing. Of course, all of this depends on the type of group or ensemble you're in, but being a "musical musician" is a skill to develop for any situation.

A world-famous drummer once told me he feels he's played his best when he's helped make the musicians around him sound good. I always liked that philosophy, and it sure worked for him!

Two terms that traditionally apply more to jazz, funk, latin and R&B are "groove" and "pocket," but what these words refer to can apply to any musical environment and is the result of elevated musicality. It's when you instinctively and emotionally feel that the music is *breathing* in an extraordinary way that almost defies description. And, whether as a performer or listener, there's no doubt when the music has elevated to a unique - or even exceptional - level.

Brilliant Ideas About Practicing

As an instrumentalist or vocalist, you'll probably spend thousands of hours practicing, so identifying good habits to maximize the results is valuable preparation with big payouts. Here are a few ideas:

If you find your practices boring, then it's within you to turn that around! Try doing some minor physical warm-ups before you start to get your energy up, or, depending on your preference, do some meditation first to get yourself laser-focused for your session.

Don't underestimate the difference you might feel if you change the location of your session to anywhere else other than where you usually practice. Try being a bit playful and practice blindfolded, or change the tempos dramatically in either direction from what you are used to. You might also consider changing the key or inserting drastically different dynamics and articulations than what's written or expected.

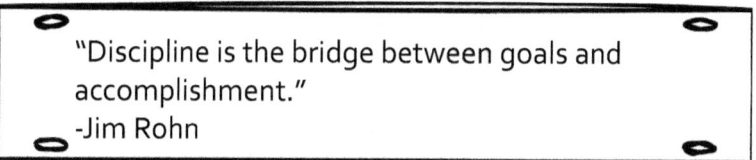

"Discipline is the bridge between goals and accomplishment."
-Jim Rohn

Time (your ability to keep a tempo steady) is one of the most valuable commodities in your music toolbox. Mistakes happen, but if your tempo is rock solid, you can power through and still make *musical* music. Conversely, if you're dragging or rushing the tempo in an ensemble setting, no one gets a chance to be as musical as they want – unless wavering tempos *is* the musical objective!

The remedy is simple: practice with a metronome as often as possible. Like any other acquired skill, you will gain increased confidence the more your internal sense of time gets honed. While it can feel limiting, the benefits will be massive, Many apps are available to help you with this, and many of them are free.

And if you're looking for a bonus exercise to humble the confidence you acquire by practicing to a metronome, get an app that allows you to silence selected bars. Given that there is "no forgiveness" in a metronome, staying steady through silent bars and coming out on the other side in sync is more challenging than you'd think.

Of course, the slower the tempo and the more silent bars you have, the harder it is; but it's a fun challenge.

Never apologize for your progress. Everyone develops different skills at different times, and while it can feel great to be driven, you still need to be patient with yourself. It helps to find humor in the mistakes and to just laugh at having made them. And while you're being patient with yourself, don't forget to extend that patience to those around you who are also trying.

Sticking to a routine every day can sometimes feel impossible. You'll have good days and bad days but keep your eyes - and ears - focused on your goals. Self-discipline is challenging for many people. Be consistent. Without consistency, self-discipline wavers.

Don't be afraid to "woodshed" (a musician's term for serious practicing), and to make a million mistakes while doing so. But treat yourself with kindness and acceptance and don't be too hard on yourself.

Are you looking for perfection? Forget it! Think about it: If you strive to forever seek improvement, growth and enduring creativity, then reaching *what you believe* is perfection brings all that to an end.

Don't forget to celebrate the milestones you've reached!

Question: Do you practice every day? Why is it you can't keep improving if you practice for eight hours one day a week and don't practice the other six days?

Answer: Your brain learns muscle memory gradually!

Some objectives are acquired more quickly than others, but consistency - as well as being honest with yourself about the quality of your practicing time - is the time-tested answer to improving.

And remember, if you have a problem with a particular bar or bars of music, take the specific sections slowly, beat by beat, and build from there.

Record yourself, even if you're just using an app from your phone. You'll sometimes be amazed at how different you will sound to yourself, and what you will learn, when you listen back to your recordings.

Why Read Or Learn Theory

Reading music is like learning another language, and theory is like learning the grammar of that language. If you read music you learn form, notation, articulation, phrasing, etc. If you add an understanding of theory as you increase your reading skills, you're armed with even more ways to make your music soar. When you understand music theory, your music is more accessible by not having to focus as much on finding the right notes, beats or chords. It's also a lot easier to break the rules when you know them in the first place!

The best studio musicians in the world can sightread at lightning-fast speed. It's amazing how they can play the music they're seeing for the first time as if they've been performing it their entire life. Where do you want to be on the reading spectrum?

Be bold enough to make a change if you're not happy with who, how or where you're learning your music. The easiest way to kill a musical drive is to continue studies with the wrong influence or teacher. Experiment. When you add up the combined indications from a

piece of music, such as tempos, dynamics, articulations, etc., you know exactly the intent of whoever wrote the music. At that point, it's up to you to interpret those indications, which is why the same music played by different people can sound so different, and why some get accolades while others don't.

Don't be afraid to take risks in how you interpret the music of others. Try tempo changes, reharmonizing, rearranging, varying articulations, etc.!

Ear Training

Very few people have perfect pitch or absolute pitch, which is

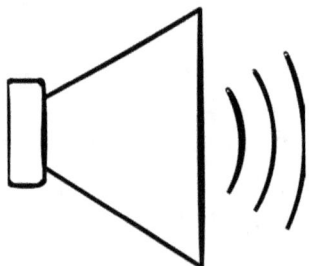

the rare ability to identify or re-create a musical note without the benefit of a reference pitch/note. However, getting good at "relative pitch" is something that can be fun and very helpful as a musician. It's the ability to figure out what notes are being played or heard *relative* to a reference note.

I know the bottom of my singing register is usually around the note G. Once I conjure up my G, I can get pretty close to naming any other note I hear. However, this comes from training your ear to recognize intervals (the pitch created a specific distance from the previous pitch).

Beginning ear training suggests using familiar songs to memorize common intervals. For example, the first two notes of "Here Comes the Bride" are a perfect 4th. The first two notes of "Twinkle, Twinkle, Little Star" are a perfect 5th. The NBC three-note theme is a major 6th followed by a major 3rd. My favorite is called a tritone, which is the first two notes of "West Side Story's" "Maria." As you become more familiar with identifying intervals, it can be an enjoyable personal challenge to listen to music and try to quickly name intervals you hear within the music.

Ear training has many aspects which are beyond the scope of this book. However, it is a multi-year program in many institutions because there are huge benefits in acquiring the skills.

The Overtone Series

This chapter isn't exactly on point with the book's main topic, but it's fascinated me since I first learned about it as a teenager. Even if you haven't heard of the overtone series, every note produced by most instruments contains them, which is what makes their sound distinctive.

The study of the overtone series goes back to the Greek philosopher Pythagoras (569 – 490 B.C.E.), who was desperately trying to apply mathematics to explain the universe *and* music. If I had known that during high school algebra, I may have been a little more interested in learning his Pythagorean Theorem.

It blew my mind when I was introduced to the series. Until then, I assumed any note I heard was all there was, without realizing that other pitches were combining to create what I considered familiar.

Let me explain a bit more - but you can always dig deeper if you find the topic interesting.

It may surprise you that every musical note has its basis in math. Notes you hear are a combination of multiple tones called overtones from the overtone series (or harmonic series). These pitches are linked mathematically, so just by listening to music, you are listening to a mathematical equation!

What evolved from the Greek brainiac Pythagoras was that a series of frequencies occur naturally above the "fundamental" – the name of the root note played on an instrument - in a very strict sequence.

But what creates the instrument's tone and character (also called timbre), depends on the strength of the... wait for it... *overtones* that occur above the fundamental!

Overtones are created predictably and mathematically by frequencies divided again and again. One half of the fundamental creates an octave with a ratio of 2:1 above the original pitch; meaning that it vibrates at twice that of the fundamental. The next overtone – the "perfect fifth" – vibrates three times that of the fundamental above the 2nd overtone, with four times the fundamental creating a "perfect 4th" above the 3rd overtone, and so on. This equation continues until your ear can no longer hear the upper frequencies, even though they all combine to create the personality of the instrument's sound.

Here is a visual of what notes emerge above a fundamental of C: Unbelievable?

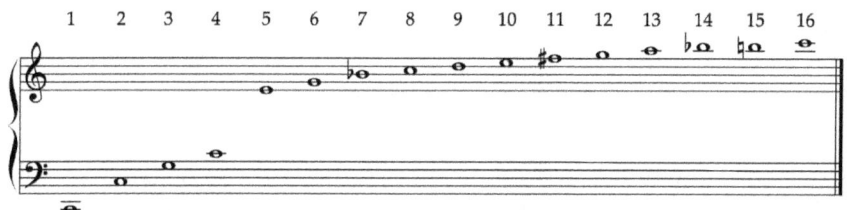

Take a moment with a piano in a quiet room. For example, find middle C and C an octave below middle C. Press softly on middle C so the hammer does not strike the piano strings.

While keeping the key depressed, play C the octave below as a short (staccato) note and listen carefully to the audible overtone. Now try it with the 3rd overtone, and so on, and you will hear the unmistakable additional harmonic to your fundamental!

You might think that you hear the overtone because it's vibrating due to the lifted hammer. But if you try it again with a note that is not part of the series above your chosen fundamental, you won't hear it!

Crazy, huh?

The Whole Story

> "You are the author of your own life story."
> -Susan C. Young

If you're reading this, then let's go into my story together and maybe you'll find some things you can relate to. Everyone's journey is different, but we often share similar experiences.

While so many of our early memories fade with age, I vividly recall the moment my 4th-grade teacher gave me a list of instruments to choose from to receive after-school music lessons. As my mom read my choices, I repeatedly said "no" until she mentioned drums. "That's it" I imagine I proclaimed in the tiny voice of a 9-year-old, responding to the only instrument that got my attention.

My first "drum" was a practice pad - a simple round piece of rubber placed on an angled piece of wood along with the thickest pair of drumsticks that must have been available in those days. However, I would proudly place it on my living room chair and play along with my favorite record as Mom sat and watched adoringly. She would patiently wait for the last beat of the song to clap and give me a standing ovation while I took a well-deserved bow.

I should mention that there is no history of anyone in my family, immediate or otherwise, being musical. Given that fact, I have no explanation for why my father insisted I also take piano lessons during my first two years of studying drums. It makes sense so many years later, but as I'll soon explain, he could not have known that his requirement would really pay off.

I played on that pad for two years before my parents cobbled together enough money to buy a partial drum set to satisfy my growing interest. I find the following picture amusing because I am right-handed but playing the drums as if I'm left-handed!

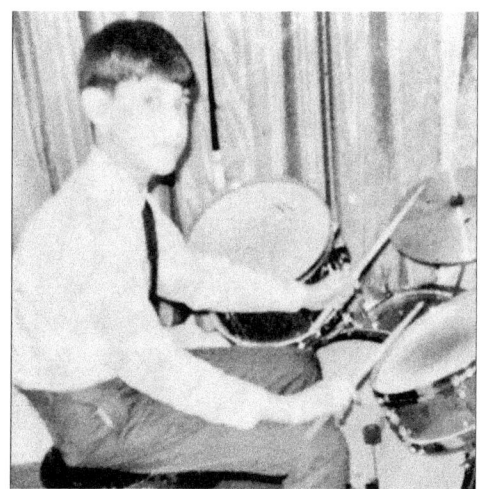

Junior High School

In my dedication, I mention my 5th-grade music teacher. Samuel Bruce was an older, soft-spoken man with wispy white hair who always wore a white short-sleeved shirt and a thin black tie.

The sign above his blackboard read "Success is the result of effort." I also remember being intrigued that the blackboard had permanent music staff lines rather than the rest of the school's blank blackboards. That the musical information being taught would be conveyed not through words or math equations but rather by notes and symbols on the music staff was a mind-blowing idea to me.

Mr. Bruce supported my budding talent by doing small things that made a difference. He would spotlight my playing rhythms that were an embellishment of the original drum part, and find opportunities for me to perform on my drum set with a talented young pianist who was very good at boogie-woogie piano. He also suggested I put together my very first band so I could feel what it was like to play closely with other musicians, which was quite different from being in the percussion section of the school orchestra.

Here's my first group:

As an encouraging teacher, Mr. Bruce suggested to my parents that they enroll me in more advanced studies at an after-school program for kids offered by the local music college, which happened to be the world-famous Eastman School of Music. Fortunately, my parents supported me in taking not only percussion lessons (which includes instruments with mallets), but also music theory.

Studying music theory was a brilliant suggestion and came much easier to me for having had a few years of piano under my belt - thanks, Dad! Plus learning music from both a rhythmic and tonal perspective really boosted my interest.

At 13, I received what felt like a pair of wings in the way of a Ludwig, sky blue pearl double-mounted tom-tom drum set with oversized Zildjian cymbals and a proudly mounted cowbell and woodblock:

This drum set energized me in many ways, supporting the notion that having the right tools can feed your creativity and inspire dreams.

Soon after receiving these drums, my parents took me to an international ice show called the "Ice Capades" at our local indoor arena. An orchestra accompanied this spectacular show and I spent the performance standing in the aisle next to the bandstand with my eyes glued to the drummer. He somehow managed to watch a video monitor, conductor and juggle all the sound effects in sync with the performer's movements, while still reading the music! Watching this professional play, as he swiveled on his drum throne switching with precision from one instrument to another, amounted to choreographed drumming and I found it to be magical.

That experience cemented my desire to pursue a life in drumming.

High School

I continued my after-school studies through 11th grade and fully expected that after graduation I would get my music degree from the Eastman School of Music and hopefully return to my Junior High School as a full-time music teacher - in the footsteps of mentor Mr. Bruce. In the meantime, I played as much as I could in various styles, including rock bands, jazz bands, choirs, wind ensembles, marching bands, musicals, etc. Drumming was just fun, and I loved the idea of grabbing whatever opportunity I could to play different music.

I dreamt that someday I might be a rock star. Even though I didn't have a middle name, I adopted the name Eric in honor of Eric Clapton, who I thought might hire me someday as his drummer. To help realize this vision, I hung a black tarp in my basement behind my drums, put on my coolest clothes, and got as sweaty as I could get before having this picture taken to help me envision what being famous might look like:

And then, in an instant, the trajectory of my life changed. Of course, I didn't know it at the time. As a matter of fact, few times in one's life do you really know in the moment that things have changed forever. Only when you get a chance to look back, do you realize how pivotal a moment was, and *then* you understand how different things might have been if the slightest change had been made.

Sliding Doors

The author Frans Johansson calls it a "click moment," but I prefer referring to the movie "Sliding Doors" and calling it a "sliding door moment." It's unnecessary to watch the entire film to get the gist of what happens to a woman who rushes towards the closing doors of a subway train and misses getting onboard. As the viewer, we see the same scene again, except this time, she manages to make it through the doors just as they are closing. The film continues, alternating between the two storylines in which very different events in her life ensue. As you might guess, the two lives are dramatically different.

Here is my Sliding Door moment:
I'm in 11th grade and happy that I have no class on this day during 7th period, so I gather my stuff from my locker and begin to head out the door. As I glance at the wall, I see the following poster (which I took after the performance to save). Here it is:

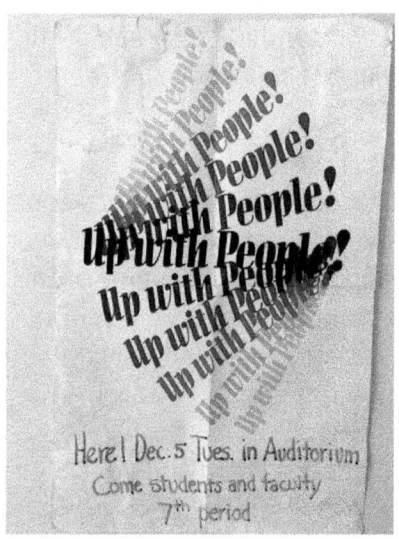

While most readers won't recognize the name, at the time Up with People had grown from a small singing group of positive American youth into an international multi-million-dollar touring production with cast members from all over the world. Although most of its popularity was outside the United States, it did find its way to Carnegie Hall, the Hollywood Bowl, four Super Bowl half-times, the

White House, and a nationwide NBC special; as well as venues and theaters around the globe. It is also unofficially credited as one of the world's longest continuous musical touring shows.

Fortunately for me, the cast would often splinter off and go to high schools, shopping malls, etc., for very short "teaser shows" to promote the full local performance, which is what brought it to my high school.

I initially didn't enjoy the show, but was gradually intrigued by the energy in the music and the musicians performing it - so much so that I decided to start a conversation with the lead guitarist after they had finished.

It was then that I found out that they recruited for the following year's production and allowed school seniors to tour *if* their parent (or guardian) and the school district allowed it. I also learned that the guitarist I spoke with had heard me practicing earlier in the day and felt I would be a good candidate for one of the three casts being produced in Los Angeles the following summer.

Two Years On The Road

With the help of a highly supportive guidance counselor who negotiated a self-study program for my senior year, and supportive parents who understood the potential value of this experience, I found myself, seven months later, barely 17 - on a plane from upstate New York to Los Angeles. I had only dreamed of visiting California someday; going there to play drums was beyond belief.

The cast had dancers, singers, crew, and advance teams, plus a band consisting of electric bass, two electric/acoustic guitarists, keyboards, two percussionists, and five brass/woodwind players - plus me on drums, surrounded by a sea of microphones, pushing the show from behind plexiglass baffles.

It was a life-altering experience in many ways, but after 24 months, eight countries, and hundreds of cities, I decided it was time for my next chapter. I had become quite aware of a much bigger world than

I had imagined from my view in Rochester, New York, and many of the musicians I played with were talking about Berklee College of Music in Boston as a great alternative to the traditional environment my anticipated future alma mater Eastman School of Music would provide.

Berklee College of Music

After quite a bit of research, I decided that Berklee was where I wanted to go. But in an odd twist of fate - even though my long-term career goal was to drum - I chose to become a composition major versus a performance major. The thought process was simple: 1) composition majors had immediate access to all the pianos in the school, which was essential to me, and 2) I knew I would already be drumming in many ensembles and gigs, and believed a deeper understanding of composition and other instruments would help make me a more musical drummer.

I say odd twist-of-fate because, as the future head of music for a worldwide production company like Paramount Pictures, the additional knowledge of orchestration and composition would give me the vocabulary and street credibility to work effectively with some of the best composers in the business. But that was down the road, and I had no idea it would be such a valuable commodity for me. I also never imagined that 15 years later a world-famous alum from Berklee would be presenting me with an Outstanding Alumni Award.

Boston was a great place to experience live music of all kinds, and I was not shy about playing in any group or ensemble that would have me. Sometimes I got paid, and often I did not, but it was always additive to my education and my playing abilities. In my spare time, I also wrote songs for children which found their way into a nationally-published songbook.

After Berklee

When I graduated from Berklee, I was fortunate that Up with People was still on the road and willing to offer me an elevated position as a Show Manager. This responsibility gave me the experience of coordinating multiple schedules, staff oversight, and quality control of the production elements of a touring production.

Going back to work with them seemed like a no-brainer since I had no idea how or where I would start my drumming career. While the experience gave me an increased skill set that would prove to be very beneficial, it did not satisfy my hunger to establish myself somewhere as a professional drummer, and I gave notice ten months later. The cast thought I was crazy for leaving before a highly anticipated European tour where we would have several shows alongside a symphony orchestra, but I needed to follow my gut.

At this point, I knew that my only choices were New York City or Los Angeles if I wanted to jump into the deep end and see if I had the talent to sustain myself as a musician. Having grown up in the snow, I was already predisposed to want to move to the West Coast, plus my roommate from Berklee had moved to Los Angeles in the interim and was promising me work as a drummer *if* he ever got work as a composer and was able to choose his own musicians. So off I went.

Moving To The Big City

I traveled cross country to Los Angeles with everything I owned: a drum set, a practice pad set, a suitcase of clothes, and about $1,000. I then bought a map of the Los Angeles area and looked for a central location, which I found to be Hollywood. It was hardly the romanticized version I had in my mind from movies and television shows, and was much grittier than I had expected.

I found a small studio apartment that had been advertised, which was just up the street from the world-famous Frederick's of Hollywood. It was barely large enough to hold my limited belongings, but I thought it was cool to be near Hollywood Boulevard. Fortunately, the landlady was willing to rent the apartment to me even though I had yet to establish ties to California through a driver's license, bank account, etc.

Day 1: I called a cousin in Los Angeles who had found success working in the game show business. While not connected to the music industry, he did impart some words of wisdom based on his experience, which was simply to not sit around waiting for the phone to ring. My cousin went on to say that to find success in Hollywood (an all-encompassing location referring to the entertainment industry in Los Angeles), you have to get out and make your success happen. Many people who say they *want* it don't put the work in and then complain that it's not happening for them, as they sit in their apartment. I understood what he was saying but was clueless about how to put in the "work" he was describing.

Day 2 – (metaphorically speaking, and I promise not to go day by day!) Given my lean bank account, I had only two choices: 1) find work as a drummer or 2) find work doing something else. Doing something else wasn't the reason I came to Los Angeles. However, *if* I had to do something else, I promised myself it would at least be related to music. I imagined I'd work in the drum department at the local music store or… well, you get the idea.

Answering an ad to play with geriatric musicians who needed a drummer for afternoon gigs at retirement/nursing homes was not quite what I had hoped my first move would be - but it was. The gigs were only one hour and paid a whopping $30, but they had so many of them it added up. The real plus was that they were so appreciative to have a young guy who could carry his own drums and didn't fall asleep while playing that I didn't mind playing the jobs as much as I thought I might.

As the months passed, I got a few more gigs by joining the equivalent of today's electronic message boards/websites. Fortunately, I could play a variety of styles, so I felt confident that I could handle whatever was needed. However, I did "bite off more than I could chew" when I took a gig with a Middle Eastern band that played songs in various challenging time signatures that I was unfamiliar with. I muddled through the gig, but it made me much humbler - and cautious - when taking on future work.

The gigs that ended up paying the rent amounted to weddings, bar mitzvahs, top-40 bar bands, jazz clubs, the house band for the Playboy Club, a cruise ship rock band, pretend drumming on a TV show (a term referred to as being a sideline musician), gigs with a klezmer band for Orthodox Jewish events, a backup band for a Las Vegas comic, original project bands, and the like. I also did song arranging for a few singers and some private teaching, but those activities didn't satisfy me.

I eventually landed a gig that required me to be in the musician's union, so I decided to join, fully expecting to take non-union gigs as needed for survival. I knew the union did not condone that, but I figured I would navigate that issue if it arose. Here's the irony: as I was hanging out at the union, I overheard a musician on the phone complaining that his guitarist had just quit and that he had weeks booked at a local hotel starting immediately.

When he got off the phone, I told him I was sorry to hear about his trouble but that if his drummer ever quit, I was good... and available. He laughed at the suggestion but then called me hours later to tell me his drummer had quit, too! That relationship lasted years, and yielded enough to pay my rent on time and put food in my mouth, and... oh yeah... it was a non-union gig!

However, it was the gig for the comedian that inspired my taste for a different direction.

Just A Gigging Drummer

The comic I was drumming for needed backing tracks recorded, so he could use them when he performed without his live band. We spent days playing, overdubbing and mixing in a local recording studio. I really felt like I could excel in this on-demand environment where my playing, *and* the sound of my drums, mattered. I began experimenting with my drum tuning, the types of sticks I used, and how different cymbals sounded with different microphones.

I started getting referred to by others as a reliable musician who was easy to work with. I got lots of studio work on song demos and even as a 1st call drummer for an Asian pop singer who recorded American music. It was then that I decided that I wanted to primarily play gigs in the studio - along with thousands of other drummers in the Los Angeles area who had come to this realization long before me, and were showing up daily with the same goal.

Remember my composer friend who came to Los Angeles and promised me work? As his career progressed, he kept his promise and would bring me into the studio whenever possible. He also made me painfully aware that I needed more variety in my drum sounds if I was going to play a broad range of music.
We worked together on many projects, including the recording of jingles, demos, musicals, etc. However, his television soundtrack to a Saturday morning animation series changed everything for me.

Enter Emerging Technology

I aspired to become an in-demand studio drummer just as electronic drums and drum machines hit the market. They were getting a lot of attention, and producers were quick to try and introduce the new sound on their projects.

My friend informed me that if I wanted the next recording session, I'd need to have some of the new electronic gear. Of course, the problem for me was that this equipment was expensive, had a steep learning curve, *and* would only be relevant for a finite period before new products entered the marketplace. Not daring to say no to the work, I had no choice but to rent the required drums at a cost that exceeded what I was making on the gig.

After a quick self-guided tour of the rented drums, I got to the studio and began loading in, while the previous drums from the prior session were being taken out. The drummer from that session was very well-known and very talented, but what floored me was the amount of gear he had been using: racks of outboard equipment that looked like a cockpit for his electronic drums, plus multiple sizes for each acoustic drum.

I had to seriously ask myself if I was prepared to compete with drummers of that caliber. After a life of committing to a career as a drummer, I really had to decide if I was ready to go into significant long-term debt and accept the challenges that being a freelance musician in Los Angeles presented.

As I started questioning my standing in Los Angeles, I went to a professional resume writing company to create a sleek resume that I thought would help highlight my experience as I explored work opportunities. My touring alone wouldn't sell me, so we added a bit of gloss to cover up my lack of significant success.

For example, I was playing with a band in a rehearsal space when a well-known singer stopped by to check out the band. After she sang a few songs with us, I knew I could honestly say I had played with her on my resume. While the impression might be that it was more than just happenstance, it wasn't a lie either, and I'd clarify it if the credit was questioned. As fate would have it, I hired that singer to sing a television theme song for me 20 years later. I shared that story with her to her amusement; but at the time, I needed a credit anywhere I could get one.

The thing is, it never really mattered. As an instrumentalist or vocalist, all the sleek resumes, music degrees and previous gigs in the world don't matter if you don't play well. When people hear you, they know if they like what you do regardless of where you got your chops from. *That* will get you more work; *not* saying that you have a performance degree from Berklee... or anywhere else.

But that aside, I continued to ask myself whether I remained as passionate about continuing on the road of a freelance drummer or whether there were other avenues to explore.

It was probably that state of mind that got me intrigued during a visit to Disneyland.

I Just Want to Work at Disneyland!

I became fascinated by the idea of working at Disneyland after seeing and hearing the abundance of music used on the rides and live performances sprinkled around the theme park. I wondered who wrote it, supervised it, managed it, etc.

During one visit, I decided to seek out the music department in the Disneyland business building and was surprised to be led to the office of the Director of Entertainment. His assistant told me he was unavailable and that although there were no job openings, I could submit my resume for future consideration. Knowing there is nothing like an in-person opportunity, I called later to schedule another time to come back and see him. While very cordial, the meeting was short, and he reiterated what his assistant had already told me.

The entertainment director did mention that they quite often hire from within. To me, that just begged the question of how to get "within" in the first place, so I sent him short follow-up letters of interest for quite a long time, hoping he'd keep me in mind. I remember even sending him a self-addressed stamped envelope with a letter of multiple-choice answers to my questions so that he could let me know the status of things without having to take the time to write me.

That letter got a response that said he was quite impressed with my creativity but, unfortunately, nothing had changed. I had found my door. I thought I'd try to sway him with my creativity, so I called him with an offer. I would, at no cost or obligation to him, help him with any immediate challenge he may be confronted with. He laughed as he told me that he needed a honky-tonk piano player who could simultaneously ride a bike through the theme park... at the Tokyo, Japan Disneyland!

I responded by telling him that I would have a list of candidates by the end of the week to prove my resourcefulness and ability to deliver. My first thought was to call the managers at a chain of pizza parlors that used to have honkytonk piano players play live at their restaurants, but they told me they had stopped offering that entertainment quite a while ago. My next step was calling on piano players I had worked with in Los Angeles who might know of someone, but the weirdness of the request wasn't met with many options.

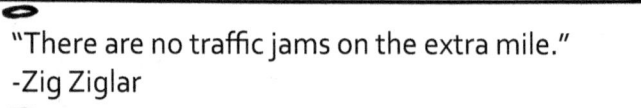

"There are no traffic jams on the extra mile."
-Zig Ziglar

One exception occurred when a pianist mentioned that motion picture & TV studios sometimes need uniquely talented musicians for their productions, and gave me the phone number of an executive at Warner Bros. Studios. That executive was kind enough to hear about my plight to find this needle-in-a-haystack piano player but told me he couldn't really help me.

Incidentally, no one could, and I sheepishly let the Disney executive know I had not been able to find him a piano player.

However, at the end of the call with the Warner Bros. executive, I grabbed the chance to tell him that I was also exploring the world of music supervising and wondered if he had any thoughts.

I had seen the title of music supervisor on many TV and films but had no idea what it was. What I knew was that it seemed to hold the ambiguity I was looking for – meaning I could possibly use a variety of my skills simultaneously.

I remember him saying he liked my enthusiasm, and suggested I use his name as a referral and call the Vice President of Music at Columbia Pictures Television (now Sony Pictures Television), who he knew was looking for a new in-house music supervisor. I excitedly called and got through to the executive, only to find out that he had already decided on his hire for the new position, which, for budgeting reasons, wouldn't be created for five months. I asked if I could please stay in touch with him in case he heard of any similar jobs that might be opening, to which he was very receptive.

A month later I called and asked if we could meet, so that he had a face to put with the name. I also took that time to do research on his background, so we could talk about him, and me, when we got together. We met for lunch, where I had a chance to go into detail on my journey as a drummer on the road, my college studies, my freelance work in Los Angeles, and, more importantly, my desire to have a "day gig."

However, what I did between my initial contact with him, and our meeting may have been my smartest decision.

Recognizing I had zero music supervising experience, I contacted a New York company that provided a lot of background music for soap operas and cartoons in the Los Angeles area, and offered myself for free! I needed to be able to say that I had some legitimate work in supervision – regardless of a paycheck.

> "You can't knock on opportunity's door and not be ready."
> -Bruno Mars

An in-person meeting with their Los Angeles representative went very well, and I was assigned a job to ensure the right balance of music during the postproduction mixing of a Saturday morning cartoon show. Although it was just once a week, it was a music supervising job worthy of mentioning in my meeting with the Columbia Pictures Television music executive.

While there was still no movement on any job openings, I continued to connect with him at appropriate intervals... until magic happened. He called me to say that the candidate he had hired could no longer wait for the position to open and had decided to take a job at... *Disney*! He asked if I could come in immediately and meet with him, and two days later I had the offer to take an entry-level position as Music Supervisor for Columbia Pictures Television.

The salary was low, but the opportunity was priceless.

Columbia Pictures Television (which became Sony Pictures Television)

My first day was laughable. I sat behind my desk in a windowless room that must have originally been intended as a supply closet. My desktop was empty, except for a note to call a producer of a very successful TV show to discuss the musicians he needed for an upcoming scene in the episode they were shooting. I'll never forget looking at that note and thinking there is <u>nothing</u> I can say to this guy that will be of help. It was then that I learned the benefit of not being afraid to say to someone, "I don't know" or "I'm not sure, *but* I will find out the right answer and get back to you."

I found out quickly who to call for assistance, got right back to the producer with the answers he needed, and was much more prepared when the next call came my way with a similar request.

What Exactly Did I Do

In case you're interested, please allow me to attempt an explanation of what a job like this entails. I smile as I write this because there was an ongoing question over the years from friends and family asking, "What *exactly* is it that you do?" It was a fair question, as was my inability to respond articulately because of the variety of responsibilities.

Let's take your favorite television show as an example. The music you hear on the show consists of mainly, "underscore" or transition music (the music that happens under dialogue or connective music), a theme song (which can occur at the beginning/end, many minutes into the show, periodically in the underscore throughout the episode, or sometimes not at all) and maybe popular - or not so popular - songs from any genre or period.

Non-underscore or transition music within a movie or television show may also be called "source music". Source music comes from an identifiable location, such as a radio/ear pods/audio player, DJ, live band/performer/street musician, etc. There is also on-camera and off-camera source music which may or may not be songs per se, but would fall into one of those categories (i.e., someone ad-lib singing in the shower or casually whistling is considered on-camera source music). Music supposedly emanating from a nearby TV would be another form of off-camera source music. Some of this music may be pre-existing and licensed for a specific use, commissioned to be written, or be part of a composer's overall deal for that project. Occasionally, these uses may be independently profiled to produce a soundtrack album, single, sheet music, video or other ancillary uses such as greeting cards, VR experiences, podcasts, streaming platforms, etc.

But how does all that music get created/produced/edited/recorded/credited? Who makes the creative decisions? Who makes the deals? How are *on-camera* and *off- camera* talent found, hired, and directed? Who obtains the rights to pre-existing music to use it in the production and for all the other places around the globe where it might be heard? And who oversees all the people it takes to answer these questions? Then multiply all those questions by multiple shows produced by a large production company like Columbia Pictures Television, and *that's* what my job entailed. It also requires massive diplomacy given the subjectiveness of the creative process, the unions involved, and the many personalities - dare I say egos? - involved from studio executives, staff, production personnel and talent.

Columbia - continued

One year later, my employee review was so positive that I was promoted to Manager, which paid a little better but, more importantly, gave me a bit more clout in the eyes of co-workers and the film/TV industry. What I didn't realize was that it would also be a chance to learn enough about the job to get me promoted again, a year later, when the studio decided to reduce its highly compensated executive ranks and promote its lower-level, less paid management employees. In a split second, I acquired one of seven coveted jobs in the Hollywood film/TV music world, as the head of television music at Columbia Pictures Television (which was soon to become Sony Pictures Television). The other studios at the time were Warner Bros., MGM, 20th Century Fox, Paramount, Universal and Disney.

While a promotion in responsibility and salary was immediate, I was very disappointed that the expected title of Director was not on the table. Being a team player, and grateful for the opportunity to have greater oversight of the music department, appeased me for a while. However, it gnawed at me that a title commensurate with the responsibilities was being withheld. I now know I was naïve about studio politics, because I asked the President of the television division if we could have lunch to talk candidly about the music department and my role within it.

My goal was to cut through the layers above me that were not receptive to my title change request, but I didn't think about the internal fallout. I suppose my conversation at lunch was smart, keeping the topic about how a Director title would allow me to make better deals for the studio and be more effective with the unions and producers. I tried not to make it about my ego but how a title change would have favorable financial and industry relationship outcomes.

It worked, and I got my title changed to Director, Television Music, but it strained my relationship with the Vice President to whom I reported. Within days, my office was relocated to a very undesirable part of the studio, away from the people I needed to interact with daily. The VP's justification was that I needed to be closer to the sound stages (where the shows are filmed), but, to me, it was clearly retaliation for the snub.

Once again, I contacted the division President and shared the unintended relationship damage, but I was cautious about it not sounding like an ultimatum that he either change the reporting structure or I'd quit. I loved the job too much and knew how lucky I was to be there, but I also wanted what was in the studio's best interest. I guess he knew it, too, because he changed the reporting structure so I would report directly to him. And my office was moved back into the mainstream, except this time it was a suite with two offices, a large outer waiting area, two balconies and, believe it or not, an electronic door closer I could operate from my desk!

Wandering Eyes

As I learned more about the business, I also realized that similar opportunities existed at other studios. I wasn't looking to leave Columbia, but I knew the shows being produced at Paramount Pictures Television were much more interesting to me, and that the head of their television music department was an older gentleman who would soon be looking at retirement.

The structure at Paramount in those days had the television music department reporting directly to the motion picture music department, so I made a "cold call" to the head of that department to ask if I could meet with him to create a relationship that may at some point be beneficial to both of us.

The request for a meeting was well received, which is when it dawned on me that it really had nothing to do with me personally that made it so easy to get in touch with him; it was my *title*. I have often experienced that once you're not in a position to contribute to someone else's success, the dynamics change overnight, and what was once their interest in you shifts to the new person with the *title*. There are rare relationships that remain after those transitions, and those are the gems you hope to find throughout your life. Ironically, this executive became a lifelong friend.

Our first meeting was a very casual breakfast at the studio's commissary. I tried to be as informed as possible about what shows were being produced at the time and which composers were writing the music. However, the most important detail for me to have come armed with was a knowledge of the executive's background, not unlike my first meeting with the Columbia music executive. Whether or not people have a large ego, they are flattered when someone takes the time to find out about them and uses that information – sparingly - to have a conversation that incorporates some of their history. I came armed knowing about his publishing, record and songwriting background, and inquired sincerely about his road to Paramount.

I went "old school" the next day and wrote him a follow-up letter - yes, via USPS - and called at appropriate intervals to say hi, to let him know what was happening at Columbia, and to express my continued interest in working with him.

Months passed.

I was very excited when he offered me the position at Paramount Pictures Television as their Director of Television Music. The job wouldn't start for two months, which gave me a very respectful window to finish my obligations at Columbia.

The relationship I had cultivated with the music executive had paid off, and while he was disappointed that he couldn't get me the Vice President title I had requested, he told me it would be forthcoming within six months.

I gave notice at Columbia and was enjoying the anticipation of my next chapter when a very unexpected call came my way. My future Paramount boss had assumed his contract negotiation for continued employment (which I had no idea was in motion) would resolve in his favor, but when he and the studio came to an impasse, he decided it was time to leave.

I spoke briefly with the Columbia people about staying, but they weren't interested in discussing any of the terms Paramount was offering – especially the idea of a promotion to Vice President – so my commitment to leaving was unchanged.

Paramount Pictures Television (which became CBS Television)

Have you ever known someone you just can't seem to gel with? Well, that's the person Paramount hired to be my new boss and I became apprehensive about the future.

Hollywood can be a very small town, and although I kept my concern about this situation as quiet as possible, I evidently wasn't quiet enough, as I'll soon explain.

My first day at Paramount started off very uneventful. Go to the Human Resources department to sign some papers, and then walk to my new office to unpack and meet the folks I'll be working with. A call from Paramount's President of Production, telling me to come to the Administration Building immediately, was the last call I expected to get moments after arriving at my desk.

Built in 1926, the beautiful two-story Administration Building is a long, narrow, ivy-covered structure used as a backdrop to countless television and motion picture productions. Each end of the building is where the most prominent offices, for the highest titled executives, are located - with the pristine lobby in the very center.

I entered the lobby and was directed to the end of the hallway on the 2nd floor, where I entered a large reception area and announced myself to the assistant. I was then escorted into another outer office, where another assistant directed me to enter what seemed to me to be an office as large as a small apartment. I could see a large dining room table in the distance overlooking the manicured grounds outside the building, but much closer to where I was standing was the President of Production for the studio, who asked me to sit down in front of his massive and very intimidating desk.

I really had no idea why I was there, so except for intense curiosity, had no reason to believe it was anything but a kind welcome to the Paramount family. After all, I hadn't finished putting my pens on my desk, so how precarious could this visit be? Wrong. It was a very concise meeting and went like this:

Him: "It's come to my attention that you have serious concerns about working with your new boss."

Me: "Um... oh..., well there has been... "

Him: "Let me cut you off right there. I'll give you six months to be joined at the hip, or you're fired. Do I make myself clear?"

Me: "Absolutely. And we will be."

Him: "Good. Welcome to Paramount."

With that warm welcome, I began my 17-year run at the studio. And to put closure on the above story, we were not joined at the hip after six months, but we did maintain a workable relationship that didn't require any intervention from the Administration Building.

Less than two years later, my boss announced his resignation, and that chapter was behind me.

Paramount Pictures Television – continued

An older gentleman with expertise in musicology was a very long-term employee at Warner Bros. Pictures. Executives come and go quickly, but he seemed able to avoid ever getting in the line of fire, so I asked him what his secret to longevity was in such a turbulent environment. His answer was to avoid conflict, accept whatever raises are given to you, and not pursue promotions.

Unfortunately, that philosophy didn't sit well with me. Although I had already seen that higher titles come with a greater salary - and thus a bigger target on your back - I also knew that I deserved to be recognized and compensated equal to my responsibilities.

Within months, there was an acquisition of Viacom Productions, a separate production company with a very active slate of television series and movies-of-the-week. Contrary to what my dear musicologist had recommended, the increased work and responsibilities were significant, and I yearned for the promotion I had been promised when I first considered moving to Paramount.

While I received some latitude to hire third-party help on music-intensive productions, the internal workload increased appreciably to accommodate the new additional slate of shows. As was the case at Columbia Pictures Television, I felt as though a director title did not communicate the weight needed to get connected to the right industry executives and/or make the best cost-saving deals. Additionally, my staff had grown to 16, and I had oversight of all the music areas required to simultaneously service dozens of TV shows and movies-for-television.

I took a shot and crafted a compelling memo explaining why a title change would benefit the studio and received a promotion to Vice President. Within a few years I was further promoted to Senior Vice President.

The new title was greatly appreciated and may have been what made me receptive to a radio ad I heard one day on my way to work. I was thinking about my increased financial responsibility when a commercial came on advertising a night school program at Pepperdine University for executives looking to acquire an MBA – a master's degree in business administration. It resonated with me and a few years later I obtained that MBA. While that degree came with a significant increase in my knowledge of business, it strengthened my confidence to take on challenges and recognize the wisdom of knowing when to involve others.

And sometimes the work you do gets noticed
It was a nice surprise to be interviewed by a magazine devoted to film/TV:

Moving On
Over the years, I had stayed in touch with a record executive I admired. He and I had a friendly professional relationship and had the opportunity to work together on a few projects. When he transitioned to the Recording Academy as their new CEO/President, it never crossed my mind that he might be looking for new senior management as he envisioned the organization's future.

During a significant transitional period for Paramount, I ran into the new Recording Academy chief at a black-tie event, where much dialogue - much of it insincere – gets bandied around. When I asked him how things were going, he looked at me and said, "It would be going better if I had you on my team." I was very flattered at the comment and wondered if he was serious. And as the evening continued, I couldn't help but speculate if he had just planted a seed that I should consider watering.

I really loved my job and the people I worked with, which is what kept me at Paramount for so many years. However, after 14 soundtrack albums, three gold records, and supervising thousands of hours of music for hundreds of television shows and TV movies, I had to ask myself if it was time for the next chapter in my career.

After considerable thought, I accepted his eventual offer to join the Recording Academy as their Executive Vice President, and left Paramount Pictures Television 20 years to the day after I had started as an entry-level music supervisor at Columbia Pictures Television.

I never thought I'd leave the studio for a non-music supervisory gig, but so much for saying "never."

The Recording Academy (also known as the Grammy Awards organization)

Only the future will tell whether a Grammy will continue to hold distinction in the creative community. To many, awards like this have become less relevant in a landscape where music is consumed through so many platforms and success no longer culminates with winning an award. However, for more than 60 years the Grammys have held the "gold standard" for success in the general public's eye, and I always enjoyed attending the show.

For many years I only thought of the Recording Academy as the Grammy Awards telecast but, surprisingly, its 200 employees and 12 chapters around the country are focused year-round on supporting the music industry. The telecast is one night a year, and while it occupies much of the organization's bandwidth, there are multiple branches to the Grammy brand. There is a significant educational, philanthropic, and health & human services component along with multiple Grammy museums, advocacy efforts and achievement recognition programs.

I tell you all this to share that sometimes unexpected opportunities may exist under the surface. I had no idea that the skills I had developed would have relevance for an organization that just seemed to be an awards show. I used my management experience to oversee staff; my experience juggling multiple television projects to juggle diverse Grammy projects; and, most importantly, my communication skills to develop and maintain relationships with 188 foreign countries that also broadcast the show.

For the next five years, I was involved in executive-producing Grammy-branded CDs, helping create the Los Angeles Grammy Museum, growing their digital presence and stimulating business development.

Until the sounds of orchestral music lured me away.

The Symphony

Even though classical music was never my preferred musical style, I left the Grammys to run a symphony orchestra, and to once again build on experiences and skills that had come beforehand. It was fascinating to learn how much happens behind the scenes to deliver a satisfying experience to the ticket buyer who wants to sit and listen to a musical performance designed to transport them to aural blissfulness.

Running a symphony is hard work and requires considerable personal and professional skills - probably more than you would expect. The reason is that, as a non-profit organization you have unique restrictions on what you can do with the money you raise or earn (referred to as contributed and earned income). And, justifiably, the people who support the organization view it with quite a bit of scrutiny. However, having an involved Board of Directors and quality people sitting on committees helps increase your chances of success, as does a professional staff in fundraising, marketing, patron services, union relations, accounting, education programs and orchestra management.

Other challenges include deciding what the orchestra will perform, which is always a hot topic. Some want to program newer compositions, and others want to focus on the classic catalog; but in both cases, everyone wants to sell tickets to the performances. As you might imagine, finding the right balance to satisfy the audience, Board of Directors, Music Director, musicians and marketing team can be very tricky.

And on the stage, you'd never believe the drama that can occur when two musicians share a music stand; whether the stand is too high, low, close, or far, or when an exaggerated body movement of one instrumentalist can infuriate another. The list is endless but this one example highlights a layer of complexity that most people don't think about.

My journey continues with this book being the next stop. I never imagined I would be writing about what I've learned along the way, but I guess that's the point.

As you gather life experiences, you never know when you might call on them to help you reach your goals.

To Sum It All Up

You've got the talent.
You're ambitious.
You've got the intellect.
And now you have the tools.
You've got this!

Now go find your place in music!

I'd love to hear about your journey at:
Youcanmakeitinmusic.com

Wishing you success and happiness,

David

With Great Appreciation and Admiration

Marc Bonilla, Dan Carlin, Marty Elcan, Bob Feldman, Kevin Gershan, Randy Gerston, Peter Gordon, Udi Harpaz, Bob Huff, Angie Jarre, Kent Klavens, Dennis McCarthy, David McKay, Bruce Miller, Jason Miller, Pat Murphy, Starr Parodi, Laura Penrose and Neil Tesser.

To Paul Ezeani, Craig Feigan, Daniel McKeon and Luke Swetland for their help in the front and back cover design and text. And to Steven Booth for his formatting expertise.

Thank you to the following who read a version of this book and provided invaluable feedback:

> Thomas Belk-Arenas
> Jody Dunitz
> Chris Fletcher
> Emily Grossman
> Pam Grossman
> Jessica Levy
> Madigan Linnane
> Felice Mancini
> Bradford Michela
> Julie Nakagama
> John Ruffin
> Luke Swetland
> Carmen Yvette

A special thank you to Laurie Deans and Joe Medjuck for your detailed comments and advice.

And thank you for the inspiration and contributions from the unnamed talent that allowed this book to remain (somewhat) timeless. You know who you are and I am very grateful to know you.

To my daughters, Jessica and Emily.
No words can express my pride for the women you've become.

And to my wife who never stops believing in me.

www.ingramcontent.com/pod-product-compliance
Lightning Source LLC
LaVergne TN
LVHW020933090426
835512LV00020B/3341